HAVE YOU FAITH IN CHRIST?

HAVE YOU
FAITH
IN CHRIST?

A BISHOP'S INSIGHT

into THE HISTORIC QUESTIONS

ASKED *of* THOSE SEEKING ADMISSION

into FULL CONNECTION

in THE UNITED METHODIST CHURCH

ERNEST S. LYGHT

Abingdon Press
Nashville

HAVE YOU FAITH IN CHRIST?

Library of Congress Cataloging in Publication Data

Lyght, Ernest S., 1934–
    Have you faith in Christ? : a bishop's insight into the historic questions asked of those seeking admission into full connection in the United Methodist Church / Ernest S Lyght.
        pages cm.
    Includes bibliographical references.
    ISBN 978-1-63088-831-2 (trade / pbk. : alk. paper 1. Ordination—United Methodist Church (U.S.) 2. United Methodist Church (U.S.)—Clergy—Appointment, call, and election. I. Title.
    BX8389.5.L935 2015
    262.1476—dc23

                                                                        2014032257

15 16 17 18 19 20 21 22 23 24—10 9 8 7 6 5 4 3 2 1

MANUFACTURED IN THE UNITED STATES OF AMERICA

Acknowledgments

It is with deep gratitude that I express my appreciation and thanks to the persons who have been a part of this writing project in some fashion. The genesis for this written venture is rooted in the annual conference sessions in the New Jersey Area when Bishop Neil Irons, the resident bishop, would direct the Historic Questions to the ordinands with passion, compassion, and encouragement. Those were teaching moments for the entire annual conference, and this teaching inspired my pastoral ministry and later my ministry of supervision.

It is the privilege and responsibility of every resident United Methodist bishop to review the Historic Questions with each class of ordinands who are seeking ordination as an elder and full conference membership. During my tenure as the resident bishop in the West Virginia Conference, William Wilson served as the assistant to the bishop. He listened to me discuss the Historic Questions with several classes of ordinands. Dr. Wilson shared with me some of his reflections on the process and encouraged me to amplify my thoughts and to put them into writing.

Robert Williams responded to my queries about the Historic Questions, and his response helped me frame my approach to writing this small volume. Both Bishop Irons and Dr. Williams read the draft manuscript and provided invaluable insights that helped me shape the final draft.

Finally, I am indebted to Abingdon Press editorial team for their critical work and guidance.

LIVE THE QUESTIONS NOW

I want to beg you, as much as I can, dear sir, to be patient toward all that is unsolved in your heart and to try to love the questions themselves like locked rooms and like books that are written in a very foreign tongue. Do not now seek the answers, which cannot be given you because you would not be able to live them. And the point is, to live everything. Live the questions now. Perhaps you will gradually, without noticing it, live along some distant day into the answer.[1]

CONTENTS

FOREWORD

A beginning Spanish student asked his teacher why she spent so much time requiring him to learn how to ask questions in Spanish. Her response was clear and thoughtful. "If you cannot ask questions," she said, "you cannot have a conversation." Language is intended to bring people together, and that does not happen if both sides make statements but never attempt to understand the other person.

So it is not surprising that John Wesley, who labored to bring people to God and into relationship with one another in a holy community, taught his followers to ask questions. These new Christians were placed in small classes where they were queried weekly about their progress in the Christian journey. In short, our United Methodist understanding of spirituality is that we must be examined regularly about how it is with our souls and whether we are making progress, that is, going on to a perfection of love, in the walk with Christ. Christian spirituality can be understood and experienced only within community. And within that community those designated to do so have a profound responsibility to clarify with believers the nature and purpose God has for them in life.

This book draws our attention to one such set of questions,

originating in father Wesley. These questions are known to United Methodists as the Historic Examination for Admission into Full Connection. They are asked of candidates desiring to be ordained into the ministry of the church, and they must be answered to the satisfaction of the bishop prior to the bishop laying on hands and bestowing the spiritual gift of ordination.

However, the spiritual steps to ordination are marked by serious inquiry from the moment a woman or man steps forward declaring that a call from God has been heard inwardly. John Wesley developed the Questions for the Examiners to guide those who begin the discernment process. At the outset of the march toward ordination and full membership in an annual conference, those identified to discern the nature of candidates' call must be able to answer after initial examination questions such as these: Do they know God as pardoning God? Have they gifts, as well as evidence of God's grace, for the work? Have any been truly convinced of sin and converted to God, and are they believers edified by their service?

At every step along the way, the church's representatives must ask themselves regarding the candidates, "Do they have the promise of future usefulness?"

And just before ordination and full membership are granted, Wesley's Questions for the Examiners are posed before the assembled conference. Spiritual conversation—from the outset to the last question in the Historic Examination for Admission—assures the church through its examiners that the call to ordained ministry in The United Methodist Church is authentic. This is not practical theology; it is spiritual praxis! Holy conversation at its core is Q & A. How else does one grow toward God's purpose unless there is persistent introspection at the hands of those whose hearts are also going on to perfection?

Finally, these questions bear great importance for the laity of the church. In their totality the questions reveal the Wesleyan understanding of ordained ministry and its broad focus on the whole community and not just on those inside the church. After all, Wesley teaches us that the world is our parish. The clergy, therefore, are connected to the whole church and not just to the local expression of Christ's mission. And perhaps, just perhaps, this book may be useful for small group study by the laity in the examination of their own calls to service.

—Neil L. Irons
Bishop, The United Methodist Church

INTRODUCTION

The responsibilities of a resident bishop are many, but the ordination of candidates who become elders and full members of the annual conference is perhaps the most awesome and rewarding responsibility. This process provides an opportunity for the bishop to have a vigorous conversation about the Historic Questions with the candidates. These questions annually are put to each new class of candidates.

The Historic Questions in Context

John Wesley, the founder of Methodism, devised the Historic Questions and first asked them at the third conference of Methodist preachers in 1746. These questions were asked of me when I was ordained as an elder in The Methodist Church. During my tenure as a resident bishop, I have asked these questions of the candidates in a private session and in public before the annual conference in session.

I was not able to identify any document(s) that establish the historical context of the Historic Questions. It is not known whether these questions were John Wesley's original questions. If they were not Wesley's original questions, the questions perhaps emerged from other sources. It is apparent, however, that many of these questions can be found in the *Works of John Wesley*. It is informative to examine several of Wesley's documents that contain some of his original questions:

"The Nature, Design, and General Rules of the United Societies," "A Plain Account of the People Called Methodist," "Rules of the Band-Societies," "Directions Given to the Band-Societies," and "Minutes of Several Conversations Between the Rev. Mr. Wesley and Others." Wesley often employed questions or inquiries, and he instructed the leaders to do the same. When the leader met with people, it was necessary "to inquire how their souls prosper." The leader or teacher had to ask "a few questions relating to the present situation of their minds."[1]

The Historic Questions, however, can be found in the 1766 *Larger Minutes*. At a later time, Thomas Coke and Francis Asbury produced an annotated version of the 1798 *Discipline*. They wrote an explanatory note about the Historical Questions:

> The due examination of candidates for the ministry is of the utmost importance. The questions proposed for this purpose, in the present section, may be drawn out and enlarged upon by the bishops, as they judge necessary; and if duly considered will be found to contain in them the whole of Christian and ministerial experience, and practice, the preachers will have passed already through various examinations, before they are received into the travelling connection. Let us take a view of the whole, remembering that our societies form our grand nurseries or universities for ministers of the gospel.[2]

The actual questions appeared on page 60 in the text, in a paragraph format.

The 1939 *Discipline* contains a list of the questions, but they do not carry the title Historic Questions.

The Historic Questions are both personal and public. The responses to the questions are personal responses based on a candidate's faith. These questions are also public because the community of faith is entitled to know a candidate's responses to the questions. The candidate's responses are indicators of one's personal relationship with God and the depth of one's commitment to God and the work of ministry in and through The United Methodist Church. The mark here is the church's assurance that candidates for ministry are called by God to the work of ministry. The people (the Board of Ordained Ministry and the annual conference) who recommend and affirm the candidates for ministry must believe in the candidates' faith in God, gifts for ministry, and the manifestation of their fruits for ministry.

Questions in Ministry

The intent of this book is to review the Historic Questions from the perspective of ministry as question. This is the premise that ministry is a multiplicity of questions that enable the person in ministry to better understand one's ministry in an effort to do the work of ministry. Ministry has to do with faith, and the faith journey is freighted with personal questions, or soul questions.

It was Socrates who said that "the unexamined life is not worth living." Why would Socrates make such a dramatic statement? He believed that personal growth and spiritual growth are at the core of human life. Life is more dynamic when a person has a deeper understanding of true self or nature. This level of maturity requires a person to take the time to examine and reflect upon life.

When we examine our lives, we are able to discern certain patterns, some of which might be undesirable. The examination of our ministry enables us to gain a deeper understanding of who we are and why we do what we do in ministry. This examination, of course, is a matter of asking pertinent questions. It is a seeking for useful answers to our questions.

Socratic dialogue was an element in Socrates's method of self-examination. Conversation (dialogue) with a close friend, a trusted colleague, a spouse, a spiritual guide, or a trained therapist can help one identify the hidden shadows in one's life that one is not able to identify on one's own. It is useful and productive to take time for self-reflection. My hope is that the reader of this book will pause on a regular basis and contemplate his or her ministry as question.

In a very basic way, posing questions is an excellent method of learning. Children learn about their world by asking questions. For example: Mommy, who made God? Daddy, where do babies come from? How old are you, Granny? In like manner, adults learn about themselves by asking questions. Adults also learn about life by asking questions and grappling with the possible answers to their questions.

Moses was minding his own business one day while he was tending his father-in-law's flock. The Lord's angel appeared to Moses in a flame of fire in a burning bush that did not burn up. Like any person, Moses was overcome by his curiosity, so he stopped to see why the bush did not burn up. He questioned this unusual phenomenon. He met God there, and God commissioned Moses to be his representative to Pharaoh, the ruler of Egypt. His task was to go to Pharaoh so that he could bring the Israelites out of Egypt (Exod. 3:1-12).

Moses had two questions. He wanted to know: Who am I that I should go to Pharaoh and bring the Israelites out of Egypt? God promised to be a constant presence with Moses on the upcoming journey. Moses had another question, wondering what he should say if there was an inquiry about the one who had sent him. In other words, what do I do if they ask, "What's this God's name?" God told Moses to say, "I Am Who I Am....I Am has sent me to you" (Exod. 3:14). God's identity was revealed in God's response to a question.

Jesus used the question-and-answer method as a favorite teaching tool. It was an effective method of instruction that stretched the faith perspective of his disciples. On one occasion, Jesus asked his disciples, "Who do people say that I am?" They responded that he was

John the Baptist, Elijah, or one of the prophets. Then Jesus personalized the question, asking, "Who do you say that I am?" Peter said that Jesus was the Messiah (Mark 8:27-29). Peter's response came from the depths of his heart, nurtured by his personal experience with Jesus.

On another occasion, just after breakfast, Jesus posed a searing question to Peter. Jesus said, "Simon son of John, do you love me more than these?" Peter's response was emphatic: "Yes, Lord, you know I love you." Jesus instructed him to feed his lambs and posed his question two more times (John 21:15-17). The task for Peter and for people in ministry is to make disciples of Jesus Christ for the transformation of the world; that is, catching fish (people) and caring for Jesus' flock. The exercise of this task is a faith matter that requires a pilgrim disciple to know his or her commitment to Jesus Christ.

Not only did Jesus ask questions, he also answered questions that were presented to him. A classic example happened when John the Baptist, who was in prison, heard what the Messiah was doing in his ministry. John sent a few of his disciples to Jesus, and they asked him a question: "Are you the one who is to come, or should we look for another?" Jesus gave them a very specific answer that required their participation. He instructed John's disciples to go and tell John what they had heard and seen: "Those who were blind are able to see. Those who were crippled are walking. People with skin diseases are cleansed. Those who were deaf now hear. Those who were dead are raised up. The poor have good news proclaimed to them" (Matt. 11:2-5).When John heard this eyewitness report, there could be no doubt in his mind regarding the authenticity of Jesus, the Messiah. John's faith in Jesus was confirmed and affirmed with Jesus' answer to his question.

In addition to Jesus, other biblical characters used a question in bringing people to faith in Jesus. The apostle Paul, while traveling in Ephesus, met some disciples. He asked them, "Did you receive the Holy Spirit when you came to believe?" They answered, "We've not even heard that there is a Holy Spirit" (Acts 19:2). Paul, of course, wanted to know into what they had been baptized. They confirmed that it was John's baptism. He told them that they had been baptized with the baptism of repentance. Promptly on hearing this, they were baptized in the name of Jesus. Paul laid his hands on them, and the Holy Spirit came upon them (Acts 19:3-7). The Holy Spirit came as a result of action taken in response to a question.

ANSWERING GOD'S CALL

Jesus calls us to follow him; at the same time, Jesus' invitation bids us to invite others to do the exact same thing. When Jesus called each one of the disciples, they responded with an emphatic yes. Jesus told them that he would make them fishers of people—men, women, and children. Although the new disciples were commercial fishermen, Jesus promised them that he would teach them new fishing techniques that would yield a greater than usual catch or a greater harvest. Jesus trained them to net people, and that became their ministry because they said yes to him (Matt. 4:18-22).

What is your answer when God calls you? When Jesus called his disciples, they said yes. Surprisingly, they did not even ask any questions. They dropped their nets, left their boats, and followed Jesus.

When God called me into the ordained ministry, I said yes. God elicited my yes over a period of years. By the time I reached my senior year in college, my yes was emphatic. I knew without a doubt that I wanted to be an ordained minister. Some laypeople and my father, an ordained Methodist minister, helped me hear God's call. It was not so much what my father said to me; he said very little to me about entering the ministry. It was his extraordinary example as a person in ministry that greatly impacted my life and my decision to say yes to God's call. I have never regretted my yes to God's call, and God has been with me on this journey of ministry, leading me by day and by night. Over more than forty-five years of ordained ministry, I have learned some things about God's call and the practice of ministry. Let me share three significant principles that are applicable to people in the work of ministry—elders, full member deacons, local pastors, and associate members.

First, *listen to God.* When you learn to listen to God, you will be able to listen to God's people—the men, the women, and the children in ministry settings and neighborhoods. Multitasking does not complement effective listening. God wants your complete attention, and God's children deserve the same kind of intense attention. Listen for the voice of someone calling to you or the voice of God calling you. Listening to God informs and enriches God's call.

Second, *learn from God.* God will equip you. After Moses said yes to God, God promised to equip him for the task at hand, which was to confront Pharaoh and demand the release of the Israelite people. God transformed Moses' staff and turned it into a symbol of God's presence and power. God sent the brother of Moses to be a spokesperson for Moses. God will lead you. You simply have to go with God and let God lead the way. Remember that Jesus said, "I am the way, the truth, and the life" (John 14:6). When the children of Israel were making their way out of Egypt, God showed them the way and led them. As they traveled, God went ahead of them, a pillar of cloud by day and a pillar of fire by night.

God will teach you. This dynamic unfolds when you keep still and listen to God. God will teach you what you need to know, just as Jesus taught the disciples how to net people. Your learning requires you to read a variety of books as John Wesley admonished his preachers to do on a regular basis. It requires you to go to school and participate in continuing education events. It requires you to pray daily.

Always be aware of the reality that God is with you. You are never alone, although there will be times when you feel alone. When John Wesley was near death, he said, "The best of all is, God is with us."[3] When God is for you, who can be against you? Pharaoh could not overcome Moses because God was with him. An assassin's bullet could not ultimately silence Martin Luther King, Jr., because God was with him. The cross could not silence Jesus because God was with him. The world cannot silence you because God is with you.

Third, *lead with God*. Remember to pray daily. You are called by God, so God is in charge. God is the leader. It might be helpful to check in with God on a daily basis. To do the work of ministry, develop a good relationship with God. Cultivate good relationships with all God's people. Ministry is about relationships. Strive to follow John Wesley's three simple rules: Do no harm. Do good. Attend to the ordinances of God. This is the United Methodist way.[4]

When one considers God's call to enter the ordained ministry or the lay ministry, it is necessary to consider ministry as question. Questions in ministry ebb and flow on the tides that course through a lifetime of ministry. Hymnist John Bell wrote "The Summons," which drives this point home. "The Summons"[5] is about the call to ministry, and it consists of five stanzas. Perhaps the genius of this hymn is that the first four stanzas consist of a series of cogent questions, rather than statements. The following list paraphrases the questions couched in the four stanzas:

1. When your name is called, will you follow Jesus?

2. Will you endure the change resultant from going to an unknown place?

3. Will you enable the display of God's love, the manifestation of God's name, allowing God's spirit to grow in you as you grow in the Spirit?

4. Will you allow yourself to be left behind as you follow your call?

5. Will you allow personal change as you care for all people?

6. Will you be able to endure any hostile stare?

7. Will you allow God to answer your prayers?

8. Will you enable sight for the blind?

9. Will you foster freedom for the prisoner?

10. Will you minister to the leper and be transformed by the experience?

11. Will you learn to love the self you hide from others?

12. Will you silence your hidden fears?

13. Will you take your new faith as a tool for transforming the world?

You can never be the same when you answer yes to God's call and follow Jesus, doing the work of ministry. As you go, you grow in Jesus Christ and your relationship with God.

This conversation will explore ministry as question, with the intent that those persons who embark on this exploration will encounter a deeper relationship with Jesus Christ and nurture a firmer commitment to the work of ministry in The United Methodist Church. John

Wesley's Historic Questions are a helpful tool that assists people in ministry navigate in doing the work of ministry while growing in Jesus Christ. This is a significant ingredient in the development of principled Christian leaders.

John Wesley worked with three groups of preachers. First, there were the preachers who were "engaged in business, and preached at their leisure in their own Neighborhoods." Second, there were the preachers who "gave themselves up, for a time, to more extended labours, and then settled." A third group of preachers "became the regular 'Assistants' and 'Helpers'" of John Wesley. They "were devoted wholly to the work of ministry; and after a period of probation, and a scrutiny into their character, doctrinal views, and talents at the annual Conferences, were admitted by solemn prayer, into what was called 'full connexion,' which was, in fact, their ordination."[6] These preachers were the sure foundation of the Methodist movement.

I. THE FAITH JOURNEY

What are we going to say about these things? If God is
for us, who is against us? He didn't spare his own Son
but gave him up for us all. Won't he also freely give us all
things with him? Who will bring a charge against God's
elect people? It is God who acquits them. Who is going to
convict them? It is Christ Jesus who died, even more, who
was raised, and who also is at God's right side. It is Christ
Jesus who also pleads our case for us. Who will separate
us from Christ's love? Will we be separated by trouble, or
distress, or harassment, or famine, or nakedness, or dan-
ger, or sword?...In all these things we win a sweeping
victory through the one who loved us. I'm convinced that
nothing can separate us from God's love in Christ Jesus
our Lord: not death or life, not angels or rulers, not present things or future things, not powers or height or depth,
or any other thing that is created. (Rom. 8:31-35, 37-39)

Question One: Have you faith in Christ?

Persons who say yes to God's call to ordained ministry must be
able to say yes to each of the Historic Questions without reservation.

1

Faith in Christ, of course, is at the center of pilgrim discipleship. Jesus, who died on the cross for us, sacrificed his life that we might gain abundant life. The Jesus of Nazareth became the Christ of our salvation. We meet Jesus at the cross, where we accept his grace that saves us from our sins. Christ lives in our hearts, our minds, and our daily lives.

John Wesley, who compiled the Historic Questions, grappled with his personal faith in his early ministry. Although he preached about faith in Jesus Christ, he felt that his own faith in Christ was lacking. He even thought that his missionary venture in America was a failure, but God was in the process of transforming him as a pilgrim disciple. Wesley, however, struggled to be reconciled to God through a practice of stringent obedience to God's Word.

Prior to John Wesley's Aldersgate experience, he questioned his personal faith. In his Journal, he noted that he pondered the possibility of not preaching. He questioned himself: "How can you preach to others, who have not faith yourself?" Wesley shared his quandary with Peter Boehler and asked Boehler's opinion about whether he should stop preaching. Boehler told him "by no means." Wesley asked, "But what can I preach?" Boehler replied, "Preach faith till you have it; and then, because you have it, you will preach faith."[1]

Wesley's Aldersgate experience proved to be a watershed moment in his faith journey. John Wesley had joined a group of Christians who met at Aldersgate Street for prayer and Bible study. Wesley provided a poignant description of his experience at Aldersgate Street:

> In the evening I went very unwillingly to a society in Aldersgate Street, where one was reading Luther's preface to the Epistle to the Romans. About a quarter before nine, while the leader was describing the change which God works in the heart through faith in Christ, I felt my heart strangely warmed. I felt I did trust in Christ alone for sal-

vation; and an assurance was given me that He had taken away my sins, even mine, and saved me from the law of sin and death.[2]

Faith in Christ is the gate that Wesley believed opened the path to justification. Having faith is accepting and trusting that Christ's death is a gift for me, the pilgrim disciple.

People in ministry are called to be spiritual leaders in the church and the community. These leaders, from John Wesley's perspective, should have faith in Christ. In the Apostles' Creed we say that we believe in Jesus Christ; however, our faith in Christ must exceed mere belief in Christ and the attending statements about Jesus in the creed. Wesley was talking about faith in Christ that is perched on Christ the solid rock. It is a personal relationship with Christ, the Lord of life, the crucified and risen Savior. Faith in Christ is manifested in the pilgrim disciple's journey that is devoted to Jesus, "the way, the truth, and the life." It is about feeding the sheep because you love Jesus. It is the world stopping to notice you because people see Christ in you.

At least two core questions are associated with the first question (Have you faith in Christ?) that warrant prayerful consideration. First, *do you know Jesus?* Do not be offended by this question, but try to think about the question in terms of relationship. Consider the disciples of Jesus who left their work to follow a stranger, Jesus. They did not know him, but they followed him and engaged in a life-changing ministry with him. Over a three-year period, the disciples developed a very close working relationship with Jesus. With Jesus, they preached the good news, healed the sick, and raised the dead. The disciples learned from Jesus, engaging in a new way of praying. They grew with Jesus, learning how to love even their enemies. Yet after these experiences, they still did not know Jesus as an intimate friend and Savior.

When Jesus was taken to the cross, the disciples deserted him because they feared for their lives. The disciples were not sure about whether Jesus was indeed the Messiah. Like John the Baptist, they still had some degree of uncertainty about Jesus' true identity as the Son of God and the Son of Man. The disciples tarried in the upper room for forty days, spending their time in prayer, listening to God. When the Day of Pentecost came, the disciples emerged from their secret place and proclaimed the authority of the risen Savior, Jesus Christ. Peter told the people about Jesus: "Let all Israel know beyond question that God has made this Jesus, whom you crucified, both Lord and Christ" (Acts 2:36). From that day forward the disciples exercised their ministry in the name of Jesus Christ.

Do you know this Jesus in your mind as a "mind regulator"? Do you know this Jesus in your heart as a "heart fixer"? Here we are not talking about the Jesus of the "old-time religion" who was good enough for your mother and good enough for your father. No, we are talking about a Jesus who is good enough for you and lives in your heart as the risen Savior.

If your answer is *yes, I know Jesus*, then there is another question. The second core question is *how well do you know Jesus?* The disciples got to know Jesus as an intimate friend whom they could and would trust with their lives. He died on the cross for them. He sacrificed his life for them and for us. This is the stuff of friendship. Do you know Jesus as your friend? In his hymn "What a Friend We Have in Jesus," Joseph M. Scriven captures the essence of meaningful friendship with Jesus. When we know Jesus as our intimate friend, we have a partner who will bear the weight of our sins and our grief. This Jesus is the friend to whom we can go in prayer and take all of our burdens. We bear a burdensome load unnecessarily when we do not take our concerns to God in prayer in the name of Jesus.

In telling a story about perseverance in prayer, Jesus taught a wonderful lesson about friendship. It is a story about a man who goes to a friend's home at midnight and asks to borrow three loaves of bread. He has guests back home and no food for them, so he thinks of his friend. Surely his friend will be kind enough to get up at midnight and loan him the requested bread. The man has already tucked his children in bed, and he has retired for the night. He does not want to get up out of mere friendship, yet it is friendship that responds to the knocker's persistence. Our God is a loving God who responds to our knocking, our asking.

Mary, Martha, and Lazarus were friends of Jesus. When Lazarus was ill, Mary and Martha sent for Jesus with the hope that he would heal their brother. They knew that Jesus loved Lazarus; surely he would come quickly and heal him. Even though Jesus loved each one of them, he did not come swiftly to Lazarus's bedside. Instead he waited two days before departing, arriving after Lazarus died. Jesus and the disciples returned to Judea, where previously they had been stoned by the Jews. When Jesus arrived, his friend Lazarus was dead and buried. Jesus wept when he was taken to the tomb. After the tomb was opened, Jesus raised Lazarus to life.

In a conversation that preceded this miracle event, Martha reminded Jesus that if he had gotten there earlier, perhaps he would have been able to save Lazarus. Jesus told Martha that her brother would rise again. Martha, of course, thought that Jesus was talking about the general resurrection. Jesus told her: "I am the resurrection and the life. Whoever believes in me will live, even though they die. Everyone who lives and believes in me will never die. Do you believe this?" (John 11:25-26). This was Martha's answer: "Yes, Lord, I believe that you are the Christ, God's Son, the one who is coming into the world" (John 11:27). The friendship of Jesus with Mary, Martha, and Lazarus transcended time, space, and eternity. Do you know this Jesus as your friend? Martha came to know Jesus as her Lord and Savior. The ultimate question is *do you know Jesus as your Lord and Savior?*

What kind of faith do you have? Is your faith a mature faith? Perhaps it is a maturing faith. This was an important matter for John Wesley; and it should be of vital concern for people in ministry. Just what did Wesley have to say about faith?

In Sermon 106, titled "On Faith,"[3] Wesley provides insight into his understanding of the meaning of faith. Wesley said this about faith: "It is a divine 'evidence and conviction of things not seen,' of things which are not seen now, whether they are visible or invisible in their own nature. Particularly, it is a divine evidence and conviction of God, and of the things of God." Wesley asserted that there are several "sorts" of faith, reflected in what might be described as levels of faith. Most important, Wesley discerned two main levels of faith: faith of a servant and faith of a child.

One level of faith is what Wesley described as "faith of a servant" in Sermon 110, "On the Discoveries of Faith." The servant obeys God out of fear rather than in faith rooted and grounded in a mature love for God. Wesley described the faith of a servant:

> The faith of a servant implies a divine evidence of the invisible and the eternal world; yea, and an evidence of the spiritual world, so far as it can exist without living experience. Whoever has attained this, the faith of a servant, "feareth God, and escheweth evil"; or, as it is expressed by St. Peter, "feareth God, and worketh righteousness." In consequence of which he is, in a degree, as the Apostle observes, "accepted with Him." Elsewhere he is described in those words: "He that feareth God, and keepeth his commandments." Even one who has gone thus far in religion, who obeys God out of fear, is not in any wise to be despised; seeing "the fear of the Lord is the beginning of wisdom." Nevertheless, he should be exhorted not to stop there; not to rest till he attains the adoption of sons;

till he obeys him out of love, which is the privilege of all the children of God.[4]

Such a person cannot linger in this posture but must be encouraged to grow in his or her faith. When considering the question of one's faith, one must discern the level of that faith. In plain language, how much progress have you made in your faith development? For Wesley, the attainment of faith is a maturation process that culminates in what he defines as the "faith of a child." He describes the faith of a child in Sermon 106, "On Faith":

> Thus, the faith of a child is, properly and directly, a divine conviction, whereby every child of God is enabled to testify, "The life that I now live, I live by faith in the Son of God, who loved me, and gave himself for me." And whosoever hath this, the Spirit of God witnesseth with his spirit, that he is a child of God. So the Apostle writes to the Galatians: "Ye are the sons of God by faith. And because ye are sons, God hath sent forth the Spirit of his Son into your hearts, crying, Abba, Father;" that is, giving you a childlike confidence in him, together with a kind affection toward him. This then it is, that (if St. Paul was taught of God, and wrote as he was moved by the Holy Ghost) properly constitutes the difference between a servant of God, and a child of God. "He that believeth," as a child of God, "hath the witness in himself." This the servant hath not. Yet let no man discourage him; rather, lovingly exhort him to expect it every moment.[5]

It is faith in Jesus that enables the person with the faith of a child to live as a child of God, loved by God and loving God. The Holy Spirit sparks this ultimate transformation from the faith of a servant to the faith of a child—an extraordinary example of God's amazing grace.

Question Two: Are you going on to perfection?

Leadership in The United Methodist Church requires partnership. Leadership is a partnership between God and the leader. It is a partnership between the leader and the laity.

Perhaps the most important kind of leadership in the church, among others (administrative, organizational, educational, pastoral), is spiritual leadership. Spiritual leadership lends itself to a lay and clergy partnership because it provides an opportunity for spiritual leaders (lay and clergy) to be on the spiritual path together. Lay and clergy leaders on the spiritual path together assist one another on the journey toward perfection, holiness.

Perfection in spiritual terms cannot be achieved in isolation or in a vacuum. John Wesley understood this dynamic, so he organized people into small groups (bands, classes, societies). The spiritual journey, therefore, could be traversed in the company of other pilgrim disciples who were on the same spiritual path. In partnership, these pilgrim disciples could encourage and resource one another.

When Jesus gathered his original band of disciples, he summoned a group of imperfect men around him. These men made no pretense at being perfect. They agreed to follow Jesus, bringing with them all of their sins, their flaws, their inadequacies, and their spiritual immaturity. They also brought with them openness to learning new things and a willingness to grow. Sometimes, they soaked up the ideas of Jesus in their hearts and minds. At other times, they just did not get it.

Jesus, however, was patient with the disciples and daily resourced their spiritual and intellectual growth. He understood the maturation process of discipleship. Remember that Jesus provided the disciples with three years of in-service training. He taught them by example, and they learned from his preaching and his ministry with people. They were involved in real-life experiences with the master teacher, Jesus. Although they were growing spiritually over that three-year period, they did not finally get it until the Day of Pentecost when the Holy Spirit descended upon them. It was then that the disciples started a new journey of faith and ministry. They were literally going on to perfection, sustained by prayer and the guidance of the Holy Spirit. They were on the spiritual path together.

Going on to perfection is a matter of journey, spiritual journey. Luke's account of the Walk to Emmaus (Luke 24:13-35) is illustrative of what it means to be on a spiritual journey that has an eye on perfection. In the aftermath of Jesus' resurrection, two of his disciples were on the road to the village called Emmaus, which was near Jerusalem. The content of their discussion centered on the events of the crucifixion of Jesus and his resurrection. Jesus joined them and walked along with them, but they did not recognize him. Jesus wanted to know what they were discussing. Cleopas was surprised that the stranger did not know about the recent dramatic things that had unfolded in Jerusalem. Jesus wanted to know, what things? Their answer was the things about Jesus.

These disciples admitted that it was their hope that Jesus was the one who would redeem Israel. They shared a few other details about the day's events. Jesus took the opportunity to converse and "interpreted for them the things written about himself in all the scriptures" (Luke 24:27).

As they neared their destination, the two disciples invited the stranger to have dinner with them. When Jesus was at the table with them, he took the bread, blessed and broke it, and served his dinner companions. At that point they recognized Jesus in the breaking of the bread. Jesus then vanished from their sight. The spiritual insight of these two pilgrim disciples was manifested in the cogency of their words: "Weren't our hearts on fire when he spoke to us along the road and when he explained the scriptures for us?" (Luke 24:32).

Going on to perfection was also a matter of fellowship for the disciples as it is for modern-day pilgrim disciples. As the disciples went about their ministry after the Crucifixion, they were no longer dependent on Jesus, but they learned to lean on Jesus. They exercised spiritual leadership while trusting in all that Jesus had taught them. They knew that they were supported by the Holy Spirit and their faith in God. They did the work of ministry "in the name of Jesus." Their fellowship was one of joy in service, feeding the sheep as Jesus had directed Peter to do in his ministry. Jesus had admonished them to remember that "I myself will be with you every day until the end of this present age" (Matt. 28:20b). They were able to maintain a daily peace of mind, knowing that Jesus was always near them. And so it is for people in ministry today.

Lay and clergy spiritual leaders are not alone because they have a fellowship together with Jesus. Together they lean on Jesus and do the work of ministry in the local church, the community, and the world. Together they grow in Christ as they walk together on the journey toward Christian perfection.

It is my firm belief that the church is the beneficiary of spiritual leaders who are on the spiritual path together. These leaders confess their sins and acknowledge their strengths and weaknesses as they grow together in Christ. They invite other pilgrim disciples to join them on the spiritual path.

No person, lay or clergy, is perfect. Wesley was right, however, in positing an expectation that his leaders would strive toward perfection. Just as Jesus expected his disciples to grow spiritually and embrace kingdom living, it is appropriate for The United Methodist Church to expect its clergy to strive toward perfection. Spiritual leaders seek to embrace a grace-filled life, one that is led by the Holy Spirit.

What is this perfection that John Wesley talked about? Wesley described *perfection* as "another term for 'holiness.'" This reference can be found in Wesley's sermon titled, "Christian Perfection."[1] Wesley also said, "By perfection I mean the humble, gentle, patient love of God, and our neighbors, ruling our tempers, words, and actions.[2] In a tract titled "Thoughts on Christian Perfection: To the Christian Reader," Wesley asked the question: "What is Christian Perfection?" This was his answer: "The loving God with all our heart, mind, soul and strength. This implies that no wrong temper, none contrary to love, remains in the soul and that all the thoughts, words and actions are governed by pure love."[3]

Wesley, therefore, further defined perfection as love seated on a throne in his Sermon 92, "On Zeal":

> In a Christian believer love sits upon the throne which is erected in the inmost soul; namely, love of God and man, which fills the whole heart, and reigns without a rival. In a circle near the throne are all holy tempers—longsuffering, gentleness, meekness, fidelity, temperance—and if any other were comprised in "the mind which was in Christ Jesus." In an exterior circle are all the works of mercy, whether to the souls or bodies of men. By these we exercise all holy tempers; by these we continually improve them, so that all these are real means of grace, although this is not commonly adverted to. Next to these are those that are usually termed works of piety;—reading and hearing the word, public, family, private prayer, receiving the Lord's Supper, fasting or abstinence. Lastly, that his followers may the more effectually provoke one another to love, holy tempers, and good works, our blessed Lord has united them together in one—the Church, dispersed all over the earth; a little emblem of which, of the Church universal, we have in every particular Christian congregation.[4]

This definition, then, describes a spiritual leader who is striving for Christian perfection and is on the spiritual path with other spiritual leaders. These lay and clergy spiritual leaders are needed to give leadership in all arenas of the church, especially as pastors. Love is at the center of one's Christian life and pilgrim discipleship.

Question Three: Do you expect to be made perfect in love in this life?

It might seem presumptuous for John Wesley to inquire as to whether you "expect to be made perfect in love in this life." Wesley would not have asked the question if he had not believed that one could be made perfect in love in this life. In his Journal, Wesley mentions the notion of "an hourly expectation of being perfected in love." He expected the members of the Methodist societies to strive for perfection in love with the humble goal of attaining it in this life. He makes reference in his Journal to people who he believed had achieved perfection in love. His expectation is confirmed in his Journal: "I say an hourly expectation; for to expect it at death, or some other time hence, is much the same as not expecting it at all."[1]

Let's take a look at the concept of "perfect in love" from two practical perspectives. The first perspective is the love relationship that exists with a newly married couple. At a wedding, the gathered family and friends often see the bride and groom as being deeply in love with each other. A soloist might sing "O Perfect Love."[2] We want newlyweds to experience perfect love, so we pray for it. Yet we know from historical experience that no couple is perfect in love at the outset of marriage. A man and a woman can grow in their love for each other. In other words, married couples can enable their love for each other to mature through patience, nurture, and prayer. To be sure, I have met many married couples who demonstrate, in my opinion, something that resembles perfect love. These spouses demonstrate an expectation that they will be made perfect in their love for each other as husband and wife.

Charles Wesley provides another perspective on love in his hymn "Love Divine, All Loves Excelling." In this hymn, Charles Wesley recognizes that that there is no greater love than God's love. We must emulate this love as we strive to be "made perfect in love." Consider the lyrics in stanzas one and four. Stanza 1 proclaims:

> Love divine, all loves excelling,
> joy of heaven, to earth come down;
> fix in us thy humble dwelling;
> all thy faithful mercies crown!
> Jesus, thou art all compassion,
> pure, unbounded love thou art;
> visit us with thy salvation;
> enter every trembling heart.

The fourth stanza recognizes the maturation of love as a process that must be finished by God:

> Finish, then, thy new creation;
> pure and spotless let us be.
> Let us see thy great salvation
> perfectly restored in thee;
> changed from glory into glory,
> till in heaven we take our place,
> till we cast our crowns before thee,
> lost in wonder, love, and praise.[3]

Each of us is a new creation in Christ Jesus, and we need God's salvation to attain perfect love in this life.

Wesley describes a Methodist who loves the Lord in his sermon "A Plain Account of Christian Perfection":

A Methodist is one who loves the Lord his God with all his heart, with all his soul, with all his mind, and with all his strength. God is the joy of his heart, and the desire of his soul, which is continually crying, "Whom have I in heaven but thee? and there is none upon earth whom I desire beside thee." My God and my all! "Thou art the strength of my heart, and my portion for ever." He is therefore happy in God; yea, always happy, as having in him a well of water springing up unto everlasting life, and overflowing his soul with peace and joy. Perfect love having now cast out fear, he rejoices evermore. Yea, his joy is full, and all his bones cry out, "Blessed be the God and Father of our Lord Jesus Christ, who, according to his abundant mercy, hath begotten me again unto a living hope of an inheritance incorruptible and undefiled, reserved in heaven for me."[4]

If it is possible to be made perfect in love in this life as John Wesley believed, what will it look like? How will you know it? Put another way, how did Wesley determine that a pilgrim disciple had been made perfect in love?

First, Wesley insisted that the person who is perfect in love thrives in "doing good." Doing good has no boundaries because Jesus includes our enemies in the maximum to love. Jesus said, "I say to you who are willing to hear: Love your enemies. Do good to those who hate you. Bless those who curse you. Pray for those who mistreat you" (Luke 6:27-28). Remember, too, that Jesus gave us the Great Commandment: "You must love the Lord your God with all your heart, with all your being, and with all your mind. This is the first and greatest commandment. And the second is like it: You must love your neighbor as you love yourself" (Matt. 22:37-39).

Second, Wesley urged those who would be perfect in love to attend to the ordinances of God. The core issue is a matter of developing and maintaining a vital relationship with God. This relationship is not static, but dynamic, evolving, and maturing. The way to cultivate this personal relationship with God is through practicing the ordinances of God—the public worship of God, the Lord's Supper, private and family prayer, searching the Scriptures, Bible study, and fasting. These Wesley also believed that persons who would be perfect in love and attend to their own spiritual formation should practice the means of grace. John Wesley honestly and earnestly wanted to become all that God wanted him to be as a follower of Jesus Christ. So Wesley was concerned about holiness of heart and life. Confronted by the reality of sin in life, we have the constant need for repentance and the quest for God's forgiveness.

John Wesley also urged the Methodists to practice the means of grace: "By 'means of grace' I understand outward signs, words, or actions, ordained of God, and appointed for this end, to be the ordinary channels whereby he might convey to men, preventing, justifying, or sanctifying grace."[5] Wesley set forth praying, searching the Scriptures, and receiving the Lord's Supper as "the chief of these means." Fasting and Christian conferencing were two further means of grace for Wesley, in addition to several others. These means of grace were a path to salvation to be pursued in community with other pilgrim disciples.

Third, there should be a genuine effort to acquire the "mind of Christ." Paul the apostle says that

> people who are unspiritual don't accept the things from God's Spirit. They are foolishness to them and can't be understood, because they can only be comprehended in a spiritual way. Spiritual people comprehend everything, but they themselves aren't understood by anyone....But we have the mind of Christ. (1 Cor. 2:14-16)

The question follows as to the spiritual gifts that Paul enumerates in 1 Corinthians 12:4-11:

- the utterance of wisdom
- the utterance of knowledge
- faith
- gifts of healing
- the working of miracles
- prophecy
- the discernment of spirits
- various kinds of tongues
- the interpretation of tongues

These are the gifts of the Spirit given by the Spirit, not earned. These gifts must be used wisely in the work of ministry.

Wesley pondered the fruit that is produced by one who is perfect in love. Paul notes the fruit of the Spirit: "love, joy, peace, patience, kindness, goodness, faithfulness, gentleness, and self-control" (Gal. 5:22). These fruits are equivalent to Wesley's "holy tempers" (long-suffering, gentleness, meekness, fidelity, temperance).[6] Paul's concern is that those who live by the Spirit also will be guided by the Spirit. Like Paul, Wesley had a sincere faith in Christ. Both Paul and Wesley had the mind of Christ. Spiritual leaders also must have the mind of Christ.

Spiritual leaders must be on the spiritual path with other spiritual leaders. In The United Methodist Church today, in the spirit of John Wesley, there is an expectation that spiritual leaders who are leading other United Methodists should be able to affirm that they are perfect in love. These leaders have the awesome task of guiding United Methodist members as they affirm Christ in their journey "to be loyal to Christ through The United Methodist Church by their prayers, their presence, their gifts, their service, and their witness." For all newly received United Methodist pilgrim disciples, the goal is to support them: "to increase their faith, confirm their hope, and perfect them in love."

Question Four: Are you earnestly striving after it?

The African American churches in the community where I first was appointed as a local church pastor participated in an ecumenical union prayer service that rotated among the churches on a weekly basis. The participants in this ecumenical gathering would sing, pray, and share their testimonies. In this setting, I observed some people who were earnestly striving after perfection in love. Many of these folk had been on the spiritual path for a long time. Quite frankly, I attended these prayer meetings because the gospel feast encouraged and nurtured me.

I remember one woman in her eighties who was a longtime member of the church for which I had pastoral responsibility. She occasionally would raise an old song that proclaimed a desire to work until the day of death. Not deterred by the restrictions of a previous stroke, she would stand up and clutch her cane, and with a smile on her face she would sing, "I'm going to work 'til the day I die." She was no longer able to do in her church all the things that she used to do, but she was able and willing to serve as an usher, handing out bulletins to the worshipers as they entered the sanctuary. She treated me like a son and encouraged me in my ministry. She cared for various family members as they had need from time to time. Quite literally, she was striving after perfection in love.

A common thread surfaced in the prayers and the testimonies. The common thread was an expressed desire to "work out their soul's salvation." Participants wanted not only to "get right with God"; they also wanted to *stay* right with God. One significant part of the journey for these folk was their participation in the regular Sunday worship services in their respective churches. Wednesday evening prayer service was a midweek event that enabled them to make it to the following Sunday. They understood that salvation was not a static achievement; it was a matter of being on the spiritual journey, striving for perfection in love.

In African American churches, music historically has played a critical role in the worship experience. In Methodism, much of our theology is expressed in our hymnody. The songs of Zion provide inspiration and hope that the difficulties and toils in this life will one day be overcome. Joseph E. Lowery, in his book *Singing the Lord's Song in a Strange Land,* mentions that the songs of Zion gave the people hope and "put us in the key of love."[1] In tune or out of tune, the worshipers would sing such songs as "What a Friend We Have in Jesus," "Blessed Assurance," "My Hope Is Built on Nothing Less," "We'll Understand It Better By and By," and "Nothing Between." They wanted to be in "the key of love."

The idea is that a pilgrim disciple wants to be "pressing on the upward way," heading for higher ground. The destination of higher ground is achieved as one lives by faith, seeking perfection in love, which is a gift from God. To receive the gift, the pilgrim disciple must work out his or her soul's salvation. The apostle Paul put it this way: "Carry out your own salvation with fear and trembling. God is the one who enables you both to want and to actually live out his good purposes" (Phil. 2:12c-13).

The United Methodist Church needs spiritual leaders, clergy and lay, who are earnestly striving after perfection in love. Are you daily working out your salvation in the spirit of Paul and John Wesley?

Wesley addressed the matter of salvation in his Sermon 85, "On Working Out Our Own Salvation." In this sermon, Wesley makes three observations:

That grand truth, which ought never to be out of our remembrance: "It is God that worketh in us both to will and to do his own good pleasure."

The improvement we ought to make of it: "Work out your own salvation with fear and trembling."

The connexion between them: "It is God that worketh in you"; therefore, "work out your own salvation."[2]

In the biblical text, Paul wants us to understand that Christ "purchased" this salvation for us. Salvation, therefore, is ours to obtain by earnestly striving after perfection in love.

In this same sermon (85), Wesley makes two cogent points regarding the full participation of the pilgrim disciple in God's salvific activity. As you ponder your participation in God's plan and activity of salvation, consider this: "First, God worketh in you, therefore, you can work: Otherwise it would be impossible. If he did not work, it would be impossible for you to work out your own salvation." This is an example of God's amazing grace that is totally unearned but a gift from God.

Wesley has another point: "Secondly, God worketh in you; therefore, you must work: you must be 'workers together with him,' (they are the very words of the Apostle); otherwise he will cease working." So, the old prayer warrior who would raise her song at the Wednesday evening prayer service understood that she had to work until the day she died to be perfect in love. Through grace she was in partnership with God, and she welcomed God's activity in her life.

II. THE WORK OF MINISTRY

Question Five: Are you resolved to devote yourself wholly to God and his work?

I have listed this fifth question under the category of "the work of ministry." The question is predicated on the foundation of the first four questions, which explore one's relationship to Christ and test one's desire to seek perfection and to strive after perfection in love. When we say yes to these questions, we also are saying yes to God and the work of God's ministry.

The fifth question can be read as a two-part question:

1. Is your resolve such that you are without reservation fully committed to God?

2. Are you ready and willing to do the work of God's ministry without excuses?

Every candidate for ministry should contemplate these two very serious and complex questions. Every person who is doing the work of ministry should review these questions at least annually.

First, let us take a look at the apostle Paul who came into ministry as a second career. In his first career, Saul (Paul) was a persecutor of the followers of Jesus (see Acts 9). He found satisfaction in persecuting members of the Way, but one day on the road to Damascus, a light from heaven blinded Saul, and Jesus confronted him. Saul was without sight for three days. Ananias laid his hands on Saul and told him, "Brother Saul, the Lord sent me—Jesus who appeared to you on the way as you were coming here. He sent me so that you could see again and be filled with the Holy Spirit." Saul was able to see, got to his feet, and "was baptized" (vv. 17-19). This event might be interpreted as Saul's ordination of sorts. From that point on, Saul began to proclaim Jesus in the synagogues, saying, "He is God's Son" (v. 20). Saul, of course, became known as Paul; and without reservation, he was fully committed to God and God's ministry in the name of Jesus.

Second, no longer dedicated to persecuting followers of the Way, Paul was ready and willing to do the work of God's ministry without excuses. Paul engaged in a ministry of preaching, teaching, and doing missionary work. During the course of his ministry, Paul was beaten, imprisoned, and shipwrecked. These passages of Scripture describe Paul's ministry:

> I'm the least important of the apostles. I don't deserve to be called an apostle, because I harassed God's church. I am what I am by God's grace, and God's grace hasn't been for nothing. In fact, I have worked harder than all the others—that is, it wasn't me but the grace of God that is with me. So then, whether you heard the message from me or them, this is what we preach and this is what you have believed. (1 Cor. 15:9-11)

Jews ask for signs, and Greeks look for wisdom, but we preach Christ crucified, which is a scandal to Jews and foolishness to Gentiles. But to those who are called—both Jews and Greeks—Christ is God's power and God's wisdom. (1 Cor. 1:22-24)

I have fought the good fight, finished the race, and kept the faith. At last the champion's wreath that is awarded for righteousness is waiting for me. The Lord, who is the righteous judge, is going to give it to me on that day. He's giving it not only to me but also to all those who have set their heart on waiting for his appearance. (2 Tim. 4:7-8)

It is clear, therefore, that Paul could answer yes to the question, are you resolved to devote yourself wholly to God and God's work? The same can be said about John Wesley, who loved God and found fulfillment in doing God's work. This kind of ministry makes a difference. Paul played a significant role in the establishment of missionary churches and the spread of Christianity. John Wesley became the founder of Methodism, a movement that spread across the American frontier. Wesley stated Methodism's purpose in a question-and-answer format. He asked, "What may we reasonably believe to be God's design in raising up the Preachers called Methodists?" His answer was, "Not to form any new sect; but to reform the nation, particularly the Church; and to spread scriptural holiness over the land."[1]

Devotion to God and God's work was manifest in the life and ministry of Dr. Martin Luther King, Jr. King became the leader of the civil rights movement that came to a climax in the 1960s. He was criticized, chastised, jailed, and ultimately murdered because of his public stand against segregation, racism, poverty, war, and the injustices against African Americans and all races of people. King adopted nonviolence, taught and employed nonviolent resistance. He came through many dangers, toils, and snares, but he could not escape the assassin's bullet when he stood shoulder-to-shoulder with the Memphis sanitation workers. He was killed in Memphis on April 4, 1968.

King had a personal relationship with God and knew Jesus as his friend. He would take his burdens to the Lord in prayer. On the night of April 3, 1968, King preached his last sermon. He told the assembled crowd that he did not know what would happen next. He warned of difficult days ahead, but he wanted the congregation to know that it no longer mattered to him. He declared that he had been to the mountaintop. In this sermon King stated his mission: he just wanted to do God's will. King gave his life to God and died doing God's work in the name of Jesus Christ. For King, love was the regulating ideal that enabled him to preach, teach, and lead in the service of God's people.

The work of ministry is to do God's will, and Jesus has demonstrated to us what it means to do God's will. First, we are to love our neighbors. Second, Jesus calls us to feed his sheep. Third, we are to do ministry as Jesus did his ministry as witnessed by John's disciples (Luke 7:22):

1. The blind receive their sight.

2. The lame walk.

3. The lepers are cleansed.

4. The deaf hear.

5. The dead are raised.

6. The poor have good news brought to them.

These dynamics characterize the work of ministry in the church today. Ministry is about serving people who need a helping hand, regardless of their station in life. To do the work of ministry today, a minister must be anchored in Jesus Christ, fully devoted to God and God's work. A consistent yes to God and God's work requires that we have "the mind of Christ." Consider Paul's message to the Philippians:

> Adopt the attitude that was in Christ Jesus:
>
> Though he was in the form of God,
>   he did not consider being equal with God something
>   to exploit.
> But he emptied himself
>   by taking the form of a slave
>   and by becoming like human beings.
> When he found himself in the form of a human,
>   he humbled himself by becoming obedient to the
>   point of death,
>   even death on a cross. (Phil. 2:5-8)

There are so many distractions that cause us to lose sight of our focus in ministry. The spiritual "Woke Up Dis Morning"[2] reminds us that it is a good thing to wake up in the morning with our minds "stayed on Jesus." When your mind is stayed on Jesus, there is no time to dislike your neighbor; there is plenty of time to love God's people; there is no room in your mind for devilish thoughts; and it allows Jesus to be the "captain" of your mind.

When we practice the spiritual disciplines, we are better able to keep our focus in ministry. Wesley, of course, urged the Methodists to adhere to practicing the means of grace. Spiritual leaders, therefore, are committed to God and God's work.

III. The United Methodist Rule of Life

Question Six: Do you know the General Rules of our Church?

John Wesley's inquiry about one's knowledge of the General Rules was not intended to certify one's ability to recite the rules. On the other hand, Wesley was concerned about the deeper meaning of the General Rules and a person's willingness to make practical application of the rules to one's personal living. It is a matter of living the rules. The sixth question is followed by the seventh question: Will you keep the General Rules of our Church? It will be most helpful for us to explore these two questions separately. Let us begin this exploration by probing the meaning of a Rule of Life.

In order to gain a historical perspective, let us take a brief look at the Rule of Saint Benedict. Saint Benedict of Nursia, a sixth-century Italian monk, wrote his Rule for monastic life. The Rule of Saint Benedict is a foundational part of monastic spirituality in the Western world. The Rule is about community living. It was a basic guide for Christian men who desired to become monks. It dealt with daily life, personal relationships, and community living. The core elements of the Rule are charity, humility, stability, and faithfulness. The Rule is about Christian discipleship based on the teachings of Jesus. The monks learned to be disciplined people. The Rule has influenced numerous men and women in a variety of religious orders who seek to love God in a more disciplined way.

A Rule of Life, therefore, has to do with spiritual disciplines. It is centered on one's intention. For John Wesley, his intention regarding a Rule of Life was to seek holiness, holiness of heart. Spiritual formation, then, is the process whereby spiritual pilgrims are being formed by the Holy Spirit. The nurturing of a spiritual rhythm enables the spiritual pilgrim to get into sync with God's love and the teachings of Jesus. Jesus wants us to love God more and to love our neighbors as we love ourselves. A Rule of Life, to have any lasting impact on an individual pilgrim, must be personalized as the pilgrim's Rule of Life and not just a community Rule of Life.

Marjorie Thompson notes that a "rule of life is a pattern of spiritual disciplines." A pattern, of course, provides direction and points to a desired outcome, which is "growth in holiness."[1] The necessary structure is incorporated into one's spiritual disciplines.

With this background, let us inquire about the origin and content of The United Methodist Rule of Life as it relates to our effort to develop spiritual leaders shaped in the Wesleyan tradition. *The Book of Discipline of The United Methodist Church, 2012* contains a section titled "The Nature, Design, and General Rules of Our United Societies."[2] It reports the history of Wesley's piece, "The Nature, Design, and General Rules of the United Societies." This document, written for the United Societies in London, Bristol, Kingwood, and Newcastle-Upon-Tyne, was dated May 1, 1743, and signed by John Wesley and Charles Wesley.

The document notes that in the last quarter of 1739, eight or ten persons went to Mr. Wesley in London. They were described as appearing "to be deeply convinced of sin, and earnestly groaning for redemption." A few of them wanted Wesley to spend some time with them in prayer. They wanted advice and counsel on "how to flee from the wrath to come, which they saw continually hanging over their heads." In order to devote more time to this "great work," Wesley began to convene this group every Thursday evening. Wesley provided helpful "advices" as he determined, and the group gradually increased in numbers. Their meetings always ended with prayer "suited to their several necessities."

The United Society evolved under Wesley's direction in Europe and spread to America. A society was defined as "a company of men having the *form* and seeking the *power* of godliness, united in order to pray together, to receive the word of exhortation, and to watch over one another in love, that they may help each other to work out their salvation." This definition illustrates the nature of partnership on the spiritual journey. This partnership was amplified by dividing the societies into smaller groups called "classes" based on their geographical location. There was a leader for each class of twelve. Persons who desired admission into one of the societies had to demonstrate "a desire to flee from the wrath to come, and to be saved from their sins." This desire would be measured by observing the manifested "fruits."

The small group enabled the leader to do his duty:

1. To see each person in his class once a week at least, in order:

   a. to inquire how their souls prosper;
   b. to advise, reprove, comfort or exhort, as occasion may require;
   c. to receive what they are willing to give toward the relief of the preachers, church, and poor.

2. To meet the ministers and the stewards of the society once a week, in order:

   a. to inform the minister of any that are sick, or of any that walk disorderly and will not be reproved;

   b. to pay the stewards what they have received of their several classes in the week preceding.

The small group members were nurtured and encouraged to bear fruit. There had to be continuing evidence of one's desire for salvation. According to our *Book of Discipline* as noted in "The Nature, Design, and General Rules of Our United Societies," Wesley said:

> There is only one condition previously required of those who desire admission into these societies: "a desire to flee from the wrath to come, and to be saved from their sins." But wherever this is really fixed in the soul it will be shown by its fruits.

> It is therefore expected of all who continue therein that they should continue to evidence their desire of salvation,

> *First*: By doing no harm, by avoiding evil of every kind, especially that which is most generally practiced, such as:

- The taking of the name of God in vain.
- The profaning the day of the Lord, either by doing ordinary work therein or by buying or selling.
- Drunkenness: buying or selling spirituous liquors, or drinking them, unless in cases of extreme necessity.
  - Slaveholding; buying or selling slaves.
  - Fighting, quarreling, brawling, brother going to law with brother; returning evil for evil, or railing for railing; the using many words in buying or selling.
  - The buying or selling goods that have not paid the duty.

- The giving or taking things on usury—i.e., unlawful interest.
- Uncharitable or unprofitable conversation; particularly speaking evil of magistrates or of ministers.
- Doing to others as we would not they should do unto us.
- Doing what we know is not for the glory of God, as:
- The putting on of gold and costly apparel.
- The taking such diversions as cannot be used in the name of the Lord Jesus.
- The singing those songs, or reading those books, which do not tend to the knowledge or love of God.
- Softness and needless self-indulgence.
- Laying up treasure upon earth.
- Borrowing without a probability of paying; or taking up goods without a probability of paying for them.

It is expected of all who continue in these societies that they should continue to evidence their desire of salvation,

Secondly: By doing good; by being in every kind merciful after their power; as they have opportunity, doing good of every possible sort, and, as far as possible, to all men:

To their bodies, of the ability which God giveth, by giving food to the hungry, by clothing the naked, by visiting or helping them that are sick or in prison.

To their souls, by instructing, reproving, or exhorting all we have any intercourse with; trampling under foot that enthusiastic doctrine that "we are not to do good unless *our hearts be free to it.*"

By doing good, especially to them that are of the household of faith or groaning so to be; employing them preferably to others; buying one of another, helping each other in business, and so much the more because the world will love its own and them only.

By all possible diligence and frugality, that the gospel be not blamed.

By running with patience the race which is set before them, denying themselves, and taking up their cross daily; submitting to bear the reproach of Christ, to be as the filth and offscouring of the world; and looking that men should say all manner of evil of them falsely, for the Lord's sake.

It is expected of all who desire to continue in these societies that they should continue to evidence their desire of salvation,

Thirdly: By attending upon all the ordinances of God; such are:

- The public worship of God.
- The ministry of the Word, either read or expounded.
- The Supper of the Lord.
- Family and private prayer.
- Searching the Scriptures.
- Fasting or abstinence.

These are the General Rules of our societies; all of which we are taught of God to observe, even in his written Word, which is the only rule, and the sufficient rule, both of our faith and practice. And all these we know his Spirit writes on truly awakened hearts. If there be any among us who observe them not, who habitually break any of them, let it be known unto them who watch over that soul as they who must give an account. We will admonish him of the error of his ways. We will bear with him for a season. But then, if he repent not, he hath no more place among us. We have delivered our own souls.

It is important to read the full text of the General Rules so that there is clarity about the Rules and what is expected of us as Wesleyan spiritual leaders.

There is no suggestion that these Rules are easy; however, adherence to the Rules yields fruit. Spiritual leaders who are on the spiritual path together can nurture and support one another. The Rules take on a deeper meaning as they are incorporated into the life of a spiritual leader.

John Wesley knew that a Rule of Life would enable a person to have direction in life. Spiritual leaders grow when they have direction that leads them into a deeper relationship with God and God's work.

An excellent resource on the General Rules is Bishop Rueben P. Job's book *Three Simple Rules: A Wesleyan Way of Living.* Clergy and laity who desire to understand the General Rules and desire to live by these Rules can use this book.

Question Seven: Will you keep them [the General Rules]?

Asking whether you will keep the General Rules is perhaps a more subtle way of asking what you are going to do with them. What will you do with the General Rules? Even though you know the General Rules, are you willing and determined to keep them by living by them as a Rule of Life? After all, the General Rules are the United

Methodist way of life. John Wesley lived by the General Rules and expected the members of the United Societies to live by them. United Methodist clergy and laity, especially our spiritual leaders, are expected to live by the General Rules.

In life we encounter Christian folk who can recite the Ten Commandments. They might post them on a wall plaque. They pronounce their belief in the Ten Commandments, but they do not live by them. Do you strive to live by the Ten Commandments? Let us review the Ten Commandments in a brief summary:

The Ten Commandments (Exodus 20)

1. Do not worship other gods.
2. Do not worship idols.
3. Do not misuse God's name.
4. Keep the Sabbath holy.
5. Honor your father and mother.
6. Do not murder.
7. Do not commit adultery.
8. Do not steal.
9. Do not lie.
10. Do not covet.

The Ten Commandments help in our effort to understand the General Rules and to live by the United Methodist way of life.

On the one hand, we have the Ten Commandments, but Jesus gave us the Great Commandment, which is at the center of John Wesley's theology of salvation: "You must love the Lord your God with all your heart, with all your being, and with all your mind....You must love your neighbor as yourself" (Matt. 22:36-40). In these two commandments from Jesus, the first commandment captures the essence of the first four of the Ten Commandments: love the Lord. The second commandment cogently summarizes the content of the remaining six commandments: love your neighbor. Are you keeping the Great Commandment? The General Rules aid in one's effort to stay focused on God's love in doing God's work.

Are you prepared to say yes to the seventh question? If your answer is yes, how will you go about keeping the General Rules? A person who engages in the practice of ministry can keep the General Rules by adopting them as a Rule of Life. It takes a lot of prayer to sustain the spiritual leader who wants to live by the General Rules. Consider Charles Wesley's hymn "Jesus, Lord, We Look to Thee" as a prayer:

> Jesus, Lord, we look to thee;
> let us in thy name agree;
> show thyself the Prince of Peace,
> bid our strife forever cease.

> By thy reconciling love
> every stumbling block remove;
> each to each unite, endear;
> come, and spread thy banner here.

> Make us of one heart and mind,
> gentle, courteous, and kind,
> lowly, meek, in thought and word,
> altogether like our Lord.

> Let us for each other care,
> each the other's burdens bear;
> to thy church the pattern give,
> show how true believers live.

Free from anger and from pride,
let us thus in God abide;
all the depths of love express,
all the heights of holiness.

Let us then with joy remove
to the family above;
on the wings of angels fly,
show how true believers die.[1]

Christ is the anchor, the solid rock that provides the foundation for living the General Rules as a way of life. We need the help of Jesus Christ, and we need one another as helping partners on this pilgrim pathway.

Wesley was concerned that the Methodists embrace what he called the spiritual disciplines or the works of piety. For Wesley there were several works of piety. Prayer, of course, was the main work of piety. Another important and essential work of piety is searching the Scriptures. This would include reading the Scriptures, hearing the Scriptures read, and meditating on the Scriptures. Frequent celebration of the Lord's Supper was another way of being in relationship with God. Fasting was also a Wesleyan practice that enabled a person to "stay in love with God."

In addition, Wesley advocated for engaging in the works of mercy. Wesley gave definition to his understanding of the works of mercy in his sermon "Upon Our Lord's Sermon on the Mount, VI":

First, with regard to works of mercy. "Take heed," saith he, "that ye do not your alms before men, to be seen of them: Otherwise ye have no reward of your Father which is in heaven." "That ye do not your alms:"—Although this only is named, yet is every work of charity included, every thing which we give, or speak, or do, whereby our neighbour may be profited; whereby another man may receive any advantage, either in his body or soul. The feeding the hungry, the clothing the naked, the entertaining or assisting the stranger, the visiting those that are sick or in prison, the comforting the afflicted, the instructing the ignorant, the reproving the wicked, the exhorting and encouraging the well-doer; and if there be any other work of mercy, it is equally included in this direction.[2]

Works of piety and works of mercy are twins. Wesley practiced the works of mercy in his life and ministry. He linked together personal holiness and social holiness. The works of mercy are the fruit of our love as we engage our neighbors in the world.

In conclusion, are you willing to keep the General Rules through your practice of the works of piety and by doing the works of mercy?

•

IV. UNITED METHODIST BELIEFS

Question Eight: Have you studied the doctrines of The United Methodist Church?

What do United Methodists believe? What do you believe as a United Methodist pilgrim disciple? These questions are at the heart of our consideration of the doctrines of The United Methodist Church. This conversation assumes that you are grappling with these doctrines and increasing your personal knowledge of them.

The Book of Discipline 2012 contains an important section titled "Doctrinal Standards and Our Theological Task."[1] In describing our doctrinal heritage it states, "United Methodists profess the historic Christian faith in God, incarnate in Jesus Christ for our salvation and ever at work in human history in the Holy Spirit. Living in a covenant of grace under the Lordship of Jesus Christ, we participate in the first fruits of God's coming reign and pray in hope for its full realization on earth as in heaven." It further states that "our forebears in the faith reaffirmed the ancient Christian message as found in the apostolic witness even as they applied it anew in their own circumstances." Note that "their preaching and teaching were grounded in Scriptures, informed by Christian tradition, enlivened in experience, and tested by reason."[2]

United Methodists believe in the triune God: Father, Son, and Holy Spirit. This belief is at the heart of our affirmation of faith. What are our basic Christian affirmations?

- We hold in common with all Christians a faith in the mystery of salvation in and through Jesus Christ.
- We share the Christian belief that God's redemptive love is realized in human life by the activity of the Holy Spirit, both in personal experience and in the community of believers.
- We understand ourselves to be part of Christ's universal church when by adoration, proclamation, and service we become conformed to Christ.
- With other Christians we recognize that the reign of God is both a present and future reality.
- We share with many Christian communions a recognition of the authority of Scripture in matters of faith, the confession that our justification as sinners is by grace through faith, and the sober realization that the church is in need of continual reformation and renewal.

These tenets[3] place The United Methodist Church in the midst of the ecumenical mix of the Christian community.

As United Methodists, we have our own distinctive heritage. Our theological perspective can be characterized as one of "practical divinity, the implementation of genuine Christianity in the lives of believers." Wesley and the early Methodists were concerned about the justifying and sanctifying grace of God. The Wesleyan posture encouraged "people to grow in the knowledge and love of God through the personal and corporate disciplines of the Christian life." Our *Book of Discipline* reminds us that "the thrust of the Wesleyan movement and the United Brethren and Evangelical Association was 'to reform the nation, particularly the Church, and to spread scriptural holiness over the land.'" Wesley fostered a practical theology and the "scripture way of salvation." Wesley "considered doctrinal matters primarily in terms of their significance for Christian discipleship." We have a tradition of striving to put faith and love into practice.[4]

John Wesley developed "distinctive emphases for living the full Christian life." Grace, for Wesley, was an operative factor in all of Christian living. God's loving action in the life of a pilgrim disciple is undeserved and without merit. The Holy Spirit acts in one's life. Wesley construed God's grace as prevenient grace, justifying grace, and sanctifying grace.

Several of these Wesleyan emphases are outlined in *The Book of Discipline*:[5]

- prevenient grace
- justification and assurance
- sanctification and perfection
- faith and good works
- mission and service
- nurture and mission of the church

It is in the fellowship of the church that we grow personally and live out our expression of social holiness. The General Rules, of course, provide the pathway for our journey of salvation.

What are the sources of our United Methodist doctrine? These valued sources are *The Articles of Religion of The Methodist Church*, *The Confession of Faith of The Evangelical United Brethren Church*, and *John Wesley's Notes on the New Testament and His Sermons*. *The Book of Discipline (Part III)* and *The United Methodist Hymnal* are also sources for our doctrine. The Constitution of The United Methodist Church has its Restrictive Rules (see ¶ 17–22).

Both the Articles of Religion and the Confession of Faith are protected as doctrinal standards. As such, they cannot be revoked, altered, or changed. The doctrines, as set forth in these resources, help us to maintain our integrity as United Methodists. Methodist integrity concerned Wesley so much that in 1786 he addressed the matter: "I am not afraid that the people called Methodists should ever cease to exist either in Europe or America. But I am afraid, lest they should only exist as a dead sect, having the form of religion without the power. And this undoubtedly will be the case, unless they hold fast both the doctrine, spirit, and discipline with which they first set out."[6]

The United Methodist Church, therefore, needs spiritual leaders who will embody in their living the doctrine, discipline, and spirit that brought vibrancy to early Methodism.

Do you believe in these doctrines?

Question Nine: After full examination, do you believe that our doctrines are in harmony with the Holy Scriptures?

This question can be answered after there is a full examination of the doctrines of The United Methodist Church. The doctrines, however, are not intended to stand alone or in opposition to the Scriptures. Wesley's belief was that the doctrines should be in harmony with the Scriptures.

The United Methodist Church tests the soundness of its doctrine through rigorous theological examination, reflection, and discourse. The chief tool for this process is the Wesleyan Quadrilateral:[1]

- Scripture
- tradition
- experience
- reason

The Bible, without a doubt, is the linchpin that anchors and guides our theological discourse.

The Articles of Religion as set forth in *The Book of Discipline* address the matter "Of the Sufficiency of the Holy Scriptures for Salvation." Article V reads: "The Holy Scripture containeth all things necessary to salvation; so that whatsoever is not read therein, nor may be proved thereby, is not to be required of any man that it should be believed as an article of faith, or be thought requisite or necessary to salvation."[2] Here we see the importance attributed to the Scriptures in the matter of salvation.

The Confession of Faith of The Evangelical United Brethren Church contains Article IV, which is titled "The Holy Bible." This article underscores the necessity of the Word of God for our salvation: "We believe the Holy Bible, Old and New Testaments, reveals the Word of God so far as it is necessary for our salvation. It is to be received through the Holy Spirit as the true rule and guide for faith and practice. Whatever is not revealed in or established by the Holy Scriptures is not to be made an article of faith nor is it to be taught as essential to salvation."[3]

As United Methodists, we believe that the Bible is primary in all matters of faith. John Wesley was unequivocal in his valuation of the Scriptures:

> I want to know one thing,—the way to heaven; how to land safe on that happy shore. God himself has condescended to teach the way: For this very end he came from heaven. He hath written it down in a book. O give me that book! At any price, give me the book of God! I have it: Here is knowledge enough for me. Let me be homo unius libri. Here then I am, far from the busy ways of men. I sit down alone: Only God is here. In his presence I open, I read his book, for this end, to find the way to heaven.[4]

Wesley was a "man of one book." Wesley wanted the Methodist people to use the Bible exclusively in navigating the way of salvation. The Old and New Testaments are interrelated and tell the story of creation and God's role in this story.

Although Wesley said that he was a "man of one book," he encouraged the Methodists to read other books by Christian authors, so that their faith would be nurtured. He did not believe in reading "trifling books." In one conversation reported in the "Minutes of Several Conversations Between the Rev. Mr. Wesley and Others, 1744–1789" Wesley made a comment about reading books. In response to one person who indicated having no taste for reading, Wesley said, "Contract a taste for it by use, or return to your trade."[5] As United Methodist spiritual leaders, we must read the Bible, read other relevant Christian literature, and know the doctrines of our church and their heritage in Scripture.

Serving as a pastor, a spiritual leader, or a lay leader in The United Methodist Church requires that one must be a student of Scripture and theology. We are to be of "one book"—the Bible. Wesley's preachers were expected to be well read as students of the writings of the early church fathers, the Reformers, and relevant contemporary theologians. In the same spirit, spiritual leaders, lay and clergy, need to read and study the Bible and read contemporary theologians and classical theologians.

Like Wesley, we must pray, read, study, meditate, and pray some more. We are to go to the study, not the office, and read the Bible. As we pore over the Scriptures daily, we will gain fresh insight into the teachings of Jesus and the revelations of God. These new insights enable our understanding of church doctrine as we seek to understand how our doctrines are in harmony with the Holy Scriptures. Doctrines and Scripture that are in harmony help us sing the Lord's song in a strange land.

Question Ten: Will you preach and maintain them [the doctrines of The United Methodist Church]?

This tenth question assumes that one knows the doctrines and has carefully studied them. The question also assumes that one believes the doctrines to be in harmony with the Holy Scriptures. The United Methodist Church in this question wants to know that its spiritual leaders, lay and clergy, are ready, willing, and able to preach the doctrines and maintain them. There can be a "yes" or "no" answer to this question. Let us start with a negative answer and end with a positive response.

If it is your determination that you are not able to preach and maintain the doctrines of The United Methodist Church, you are left with three plausible options. First, if there is a doctrine that you believe is not in harmony with the Scriptures, it would be helpful to take this doctrine to God in prayer, asking God to provide you with insight and wisdom on the matter, helping you learn the harmony. Study the doctrine thoroughly in light of its scriptural foundation and basis. Talk with another pilgrim disciple about the meaning of the doctrine and its harmony with the Scriptures. Read the appropriate scriptures together and discuss them. Ask God to help you illumine the harmony, hear the harmony, and speak the harmony. When you achieve a new understanding of the harmony in your head and heart, you will be ready to preach the doctrine and maintain it.

Second, if there is a doctrine that you believe is not in harmony with the Scriptures, you could seek to have the doctrine changed, providing that it is not under the language of our Restrictive Rules. Every United Methodist member has the right to petition the General Conference to change our theological position on various matters.

The third option I regard as a last resort. If you disagree with parts of our doctrines and you under no circumstances can preach and maintain them, it is time for you to find a new church home in another denomination. For example, if you do not accept infant baptism, you should seek a more compatible denomination. Another example is the open Communion table. If you do not agree with this practice, you should seek a new church home. Let us examine a more critical doctrine. If you do not believe in the resurrection of Jesus Christ, a new church home is the place for you.

As a United Methodist minister, one should personally have studied the doctrines of the church. They constitute our beliefs. To effectively serve in The United Methodist Church, one needs to affirm that the doctrines are in harmony with the Scriptures. It is at this point that one can preach the doctrines and maintain them.

We maintain the doctrines by teaching the congregation about the doctrines and what they mean in relationship to the Bible. Bishop Kenneth Carder has written a useful resource, *The United Methodist Way: Living Our Beliefs*. Another resource is Bishop William H. Willimon's *United Methodist Beliefs*. It is always in order to engage the laity in a study of *The Book of Discipline*. In the local church small group discussions could be devoted to the study of our beliefs and doctrines. A Bible study group might want to study the meaning of baptism in light of the relevant biblical texts. Another topic might be the doctrine of salvation as illustrated in the Bible. These are a few illustrations of how we can maintain our doctrines.

When a person in ministry says yes to our doctrines, that person can preach the doctrines with power and authority. There is no authenticity in a preacher preaching on a subject that he or she does not believe in as a basic belief. The various United Methodist beliefs lend themselves to a sermon series or a single sermon. Preaching should be proclamation as well as a teaching event.

What will you do with the doctrines of The United Methodist Church? I encourage you to take our doctrines and share them:

- Affirm our doctrines.
- Teach our doctrines.
- Preach our doctrines.
- Live by our doctrines.

This is the United Methodist way.

V. Connectionalism, Governance, and Polity

Question Eleven: Have you studied our form of church discipline and polity?

At first glance, this seems to be a simple question, but it is more complex than a "yes" or "no" answer. This eleventh question raises two additional queries. What do we mean by *church discipline*? What is meant by the term *polity*?

What is church discipline? The United Methodist Church in its wisdom chose to place its rules in a book of discipline rather than a book of laws. This is appropriate because *The Book of Discipline of The United Methodist Church* contains the covenants by which we have agreed to live together. These covenants (rules, laws, policies) govern our life together in community as a connectional church. We are held together in community by the covenants. These covenants order our life together as a connectional church.

Church discipline, therefore, is based on the Scriptures. Church discipline might be described as a code of conduct. How will we conduct ourselves in matters of the church? What will be our conduct in the arenas of evangelism, stewardship, education, administration, worship, and missions? Our conduct in all matters of the church should always be guided by the Scriptures.

Church discipline has to do with accountability. We are accountable to one another, but ultimately, we are accountable to God in all matters of church discipline. Several years ago, an irate United Methodist called my office wanting to know who is over the bishop. My administrative secretary told this caller that God is over the bishop. I could not have given a better response because ultimately I am accountable to God. Church discipline requires that we practice the spiritual disciplines in order that we might love God and do God's work.

What is church polity? Church polity has to do with the political organization of the church. The United Methodist Church has a peculiar polity or system of governance. There is no head of the communion or denomination. The General Conference is the policy-making body in the denomination. The Judicial Council is the denomination's supreme court. The Council of Bishops provides oversight and supervision in the denomination. The boards and agencies are the programmatic arm of the denomination. We have an episcopal form of government that allows bishops to appoint pastors to local churches. The polity of The United Methodist Church is set forth in *The Book of Discipline*, which undergoes review and revision every four years.

John Wesley was an organizational genius who viewed church government and polity as a means of grace. Wesley provides his insight on the matter of discipline in his sermon "On God's Vineyard." The sermon is based on Isaiah 5:4: "What more was there to do for my vineyard that I haven't done for it? / When I expected it to grow good grapes, why did it grow rotten grapes?" Wesley is concerned about God's activity in the Methodist vineyard and the need for Methodists to work with God in bearing good fruit. He states:

> Nothing can be more simple, nothing more rational, than the Methodist discipline: It is entirely founded on common sense, particularly applying the general rules of Scripture. Any person determined to save his soul may be united (this is the only condition required) with them. But this desire must be evidenced by three marks: Avoiding all known sin; doing good after his power; and, attending all the ordinances of God. He is then placed in such a class as is convenient for him, where he spends about an hour in a week. And, the next quarter, if nothing is objected to him, he is admitted into the society: And therein he may continue as long as he continues to meet his brethren, and walks according to his profession.[1]

One might say that The United Methodist Church is "organized to beat the devil," within and without. Wesley was always concerned about saving souls. Discipline for Wesley was about "applying the general rules of Scripture."

Question Twelve: Do you approve of our church government and polity?

Church government is a necessary reality that facilitates order in the life of the church. Church government provides for appropriate authority and helpful organization that enable ministry and mission. From the perspective of the New Testament, Jesus is the head of the church (Col. 1:18).

The forms of church governance in Christendom can be described in at least three general categories. The first form is an episcopal polity, which is the form of government used in The United

Methodist Church. The bishop is the chief leader who works in concert with other leaders (lay and clergy) as well as a variety of agencies. The General Conference is the main legislative body, and the annual conference is the basic unit of the denomination.

Second, there is the presbyterian form of church government, in which the board of elders holds the basic power and authority.

The third form of church government is the congregational form, with power and authority lodged in the local congregation. It is an autonomous form of government.

The twelfth question wants to know whether you approve our episcopal form of church government and polity. The word *approve* means "to accept, appreciate, and commend" among other synonyms. To approve our form of church government means that one is willing to live with this form of government. It further means that one is willing to do ministry in the context of The United Methodist Church and on behalf of the denomination without reservation.

For John Wesley, it can be argued that his focus was on spiritual holiness and the mission of the church. Church leaders need to embrace and live out spiritual holiness as they carry out the church's mission. Church government and polity are means or vehicles that aid in carrying out the church's mission.

Our church leaders must remind the whole church about its mission. In plain language, "the mission of the Church is to make disciples of Jesus Christ for the transformation of the world." In direct relationship to this mission, *The Book of Discipline* states, "Local churches provide the most significant arena through which disciple-making occurs."[1] Our polity undergirds the mission and ministry of The United Methodist Church.[2] Our disciple making, therefore, has two foci:

- proclaiming the good news of God's grace
- exemplifying Jesus' command to love God and neighbor

In saying yes to our church government and polity, we give approval to the ministry of all Christians through the government and polity of our United Methodist Church. Our polity is not only a means of grace; it is also an instrument that facilitates ministry and mission.

Those persons who approve our church government and polity have the opportunity to affirm it, institute it, and live with it as a means of ministry and mission.

Question Thirteen: Will you support and maintain them [our church government and polity]?

Having studied and approved our United Methodist Church doctrine and polity, we have the ongoing task to support and maintain them. When we see our polity as a means of grace and church government facilitates ministry and mission, we then can readily support our church government and polity.

Although Wesley asked whether one is willing to support and maintain our church government and polity, we should not be blind in our support. We should ask appropriate questions about our church government and polity. Does our church government facilitate the church's ministry and mission? Does our polity facilitate holiness and commitment to missions? The answer to these fundamental questions should be an emphatic yes. In our leadership, can we help to enhance this process?

Polity must always undergird the church's mission "to make disciples of Jesus Christ for the transformation of the world." There are times, however, when one might conclude that a change in church government is in order. There are appropriate ways, of course, to go about bringing changes in church government and polity. On the other hand, there are possibilities for engaging our government and polity in creative and useful ways. Our polity should enable ministry and mission, not hinder them.

The local church is central to our ministry and mission in the Wesleyan spirit. "Under the discipline of the Holy Spirit, the church exists for the maintenance of worship, the edification of believers, and the redemption of the world."[1] Through the local churches, The United Methodist Church encounters the world. The structures of society are engaged by Christians who disperse from local churches, the strategic base. "The function of the local church, under the guidance of the Holy Spirit, is to help people to accept and confess Jesus Christ as Lord and Savior and to live their daily lives in light of their relationship with God."[2] The local church is a staging area for ministry and mission. Ultimately, it is not the structures, governance, organization, or polity that delivers ministry and mission; it is the local church.

With this in mind,

> the local church shall be organized so that it can pursue its primary task and mission in the context of its own community—reaching out and receiving with joy all who will respond; encouraging people in their relationship with God and inviting them to commitment to God's love in Jesus Christ; providing opportunities for them to seek strengthening and growth in spiritual formation; and supporting them to live lovingly and justly in the power of the Holy Spirit as faithful disciples.[3]

After caring for the required organizational responsibilities in fulfilling its primary task, a local church can then incorporate creativity and ingenuity into its organizational plan. Certain basic units are required; however, our polity allows for a certain amount of flexibility.

There is enough creative proximity in our polity to allow creative leaders to think outside the box. We should not accuse our church government of placing limitations on our organizational possibilities as we organize to carry out the mission of the church. Our commitment is to support and maintain our church government and polity as we do God's work. We have innumerable opportunities while leading to unearth the creative possibilities.

VI. The Practice of Ministry

Question Fourteen: Will you diligently instruct the children in every place?

Do you like children? No, do you love children? If you do not love children, there is no place for you in the ordained ministry of The United Methodist Church. I firmly believe that people in ministry must love children and love all of God's people; otherwise, you should enter a profession where you do not have to relate directly with people, especially children. Ministry is with people, and it is about relationships.

Jesus loved children, and he taught the disciples about the supreme importance of children. One day people were bringing their little children to Jesus so that he could touch them. The disciples, however, spoke sternly to the parents and their children. When Jesus noticed what was going on, he was indignant and told them: "Don't forbid them, because God's kingdom belongs to people like these children" (Mark 10:14). First, Jesus taught the disciples to love children and never stand between him and children. Second, Jesus taught the disciples that a person must receive the kingdom of God as a little child. On this occasion, after this incident, Jesus took the children in his arms and blessed them.

Clare Herbert Woolston (1856–1927) wrote the hymn "Jesus Loves the Little Children."[1] This is a favorite hymn, especially among children, and rightly so. All of God's children are precious, regardless of their race, color, nationality, or economic standing. Children are our most precious gift, and the church has a responsibility to care for them. Ministers, therefore, are charged with the responsibility of instructing the children in partnership with the laity.

During my seminary years, I served as a helper in my local church's vacation Bible school. When I was a pastor, I had the great experience to serve as a Sunday school teacher. It provided an opportunity to get to know children. One special opportunity for a pastor to instruct children is in the confirmation class. It is my belief that a pastor should not delegate this task but assume full responsibility for teaching the confirmation class. Confirmation class provides an excellent opportunity for the pastor to team with a layperson in teaching the class.

The pastoral leader who takes seriously the task of "instructing the children" will seize the opportunity to help the local church become known in the community as a place where children are welcome. The local church should be known as a safe sanctuary; a place where children become shiny new Christians. These churches where children are welcome and safe provide opportunities for children

- to learn
- to play
- to experience Christian fellowship
- to grow in Jesus Christ
- to become pilgrim disciples

The pastoral leader in these sanctuaries will know the children by name, and he or she will be known by the children. The children will come to know the pastoral leader as teacher and friend. Such a pastoral leader also will know the congregation's children and the neighborhood children—especially the neighborhood children.

It has been my experience in pastoral ministry that children have a way of bringing their parents and family to church with them. At first, it might be that the adults simply come to see what their children are doing at church. Then these same adults in time might come to church to see what the church can do for them. Be patient and open to receiving children and their parents. Children also will bring their friends to church with them. I have met some very fine child evangelists over the years.

Let us be diligent and intentional about instructing children in every place. In today's world, every place extends far beyond the church building. Every place might include the neighborhood schools, the community center, the YMCA or YWCA, the Boys' Club or Girls' Club, the volunteer firehouse, or wherever children gather.

Question Fifteen: Will you visit from house to house?

Although some people miss the days when doctors made house calls, still other folk remember the days when pastors made house calls or visited from house to house. Today we go to the doctor's office when we are sick, and if there is a medical emergency, we go to the emergency room. When I was growing up, family physicians in the various cities where we lived made house calls. Time has brought about a change, and most doctors do not make house calls. The practice of medicine has changed with many physicians working in a specialized field, and family physicians are perhaps too busy to make house calls.

There also was a time when pastors regularly made house calls in the spirit of John Wesley. A pastor would sometimes make an appointment with a family but most often would simply drop in for a visit. The home visit was a standard pastoral care strategy. It also was a visitation evangelism tool. Pastors are not making home visits with the same enthusiasm and regularity as they did a generation ago. A frequent complaint expressed by laity is that the pastor does not visit from door to door. Some pastors are accused of not even visiting people who are sick and unable to leave their homes.

Does a home visit have any value? A home visit provides an opportunity for the pastor and parishioner to have an informal conversation in a nonthreatening setting—the parishioner's home. A pastor gets to see a parishioner's home life as it is in the context of a particular family's reality. Often, very healthy friendships develop from pastoral home visits. At minimum, a pastor and a parishioner might develop a relationship that is difficult to cultivate when the only contact is limited to the church building.

Yet certain realities tend to mitigate against the pastoral home visit today. One reality is that few people are at home because most folk are employed outside the home. Pastors are cautious about home visits because of the potential for sexual harassment complaints. The technological age also has a way of undermining home visits, when a pastor can e-mail, text, tweet, or make a phone call. Some pastors seem to be uncomfortable making home visits, while others seem not to have time for home visits. Still others see no value in making home visits.

It might be that the home visit is no longer the first response in a pastor's care of his or her congregation. I believe, however, that it is appropriate for pastors to visit from house to house in today's culture with all of its limitations. There is no substitute for personal contact with one's parishioners; however, one must understand local culture and govern oneself accordingly.

The core issue here is this: how does a pastor visit from house to house in light of all of the prevailing cultural limitations and possibilities? Let us consider some possibilities:

- Visit from house to house in all the places where this is acceptable to your parishioners.
- Use the telephone to call people and let them know that you are thinking of them.
- Invite small groups to come to the parsonage for dessert and conversation.
- Have a breakfast meeting with a small group of people.
- Visit people at their work site by appointment.
- Go to the places where people gather in your community—post office, general store, volunteer firehouse, and so on.
- Go to places where young people gather—sporting events, school plays, concerts.
- Make contact with the small groups that are a part of the church's program.
- Participate in town meetings and community events.
- Cautiously use social media as a means of communication with people.
- Get involved personally in an ongoing community project.
- Join a civic club or participate as a volunteer in a community organization.

At any rate, get out of your easy chair and be among all the people you can encounter. Talk with people, and listen to their stories. Follow the leading of the Holy Spirit as you meander among God's people in the church and in the community.

Christ sends his ministers into the world. John Wesley wanted the Methodists to "spread scriptural holiness over the land"[1] as a primary task. So, we go from house to house, knocking on doors, ringing doorbells, and sharing the good news.

Question Sixteen: Will you recommend fasting or abstinence, both by precept and example?

Fasting, although biblical and Wesleyan, is not widely practiced in United Methodist circles today. John Wesley personally fasted weekly, and he recommended fasting as a means of grace.

Wesley provided valuable insight into his understanding of fasting in this sermon, "Sermon on the Mount":

> But of all the means of grace there is scarce any concerning which men have run into greater extremes, than that of which our Lord speaks in the above-mentioned words, I mean religious fasting. How have some exalted this beyond all Scripture and reason; and others utterly disregarded it; as it were, revenging themselves by undervaluing as much as the former had overvalued it! Those have spoken of it, as if it were all in all; if not the end itself, yet infallibly connected with it: These, as if it were just nothing, as if it were a fruitless labour, which had no relation at all thereto. Whereas it is certain the truth lies between them both. It is not all, nor yet is it nothing. It is not the end, but it is a precious means thereto; a means which God himself has ordained, and in which therefore, when it is duly used, he will surely give us his blessing.[1]

He provided guidance on the frequency of one's fasting:

> As to the degrees or measures of fasting, we have instances of some who have fasted several days together. So Moses, Elijah, and our blessed Lord, being endued with supernatural strength for that purpose, are recorded to have fasted, without intermission, "forty days and forty nights." But the time of fasting, more frequently

mentioned in Scripture, is one day, from morning till evening. And this was the fast commonly observed among
the ancient Christians. But beside these, they had also
their half-fasts (Semijejunia, as Tertullian styles them) on
the fourth and sixth days of the week, (Wednesday and
Friday,) throughout the year; on which they took no sus-
tenance till three in the afternoon, the time when they returned from the public service.[2]

Wesley would begin his fast on Thursday evening and continue to
the late afternoon on Friday, about twenty-four hours. Is there any
difference between fasting and abstinence? Wesley said,

Nearly related to this, is what our Church seems peculiar-
ly to mean by the term abstinence; which may be used
when we cannot fast entirely, by reason of sickness or
bodily weakness. This is the eating little; the abstaining in
part; the taking a smaller quantity of food than usual. I do
not remember any scriptural instance of this. But neither
can I condemn it.[3]

Why should we fast? Fasting can be a means of overcoming sin.
One reason for fasting, then, is to eradicate one's sin:

Here, then, is the natural ground of fasting. One who is
under deep affliction, overwhelmed with sorrow for sin,
and a strong apprehension of the wrath of God, would,
without any rule, without knowing or considering whether it were a command of God or not, "forget to eat his
bread," abstain not only from pleasant but even from
needful food;—like St. Paul, who, after he was led into
Damascus, "was three days without sight, and did neither
eat nor drink." (Acts 9:9)[4]

Wesley also linked fasting and prayer. Consider this insight:

> A Fifth and more weighty reason for fasting is, that it is an help to prayer; particularly when we set apart larger portions of time for private prayer. Then especially it is that God is often pleased to lift up the souls of his servants above all the things of earth, and sometimes to rap them up, as it were, into the third heavens. And it is chiefly, as it is an help to prayer, that it has so frequently been found a means, in the hand of God, of confirming and increasing, not one virtue, not chastity only, (as some have idly imagined, without any ground either from Scripture, reason, or experience,) but also seriousness of spirit, earnestness, sensibility and tenderness of conscience, deadness to the world, and consequently the love of God, and every holy and heavenly affection.[5]

Wesley regarded fasting as a part of the biblical tradition. Jesus, our mentor, engaged in fasting. His fasting brought him closer to God. The practice of fasting and abstinence can be a means of bringing the pilgrim disciple closer to God. As we grow in our relationship with Christ, we develop a more mature relationship with God. In our fasting we grow to be more like Jesus.

This kind of fasting requires us to discern what it is that so often separates us from God. Isaiah 58 helps the pilgrim disciple discern what separates us from God:

> Is this what you call a fast,
> a day acceptable to the LORD?
> Isn't this the fast I choose:
> releasing wicked restraints, untying the ropes of a yoke,
> setting free the mistreated,

and breaking every yoke?
Isn't it sharing your bread with the hungry
and bringing the homeless poor into your house,
covering the naked when you see them,
and not hiding from your own family? (Isa. 58:5c-7)

When we fail to carry out God's desire, we separate ourselves
from God. Fasting can eliminate these barriers that separate us from
God. Ann Weems calls this a "fasting of the heart."[6] This kind of
fasting requires us to give up anything that prohibits us from loving
our neighbors as we love ourselves. Weems opts for us to live God's
story rather than live our own stories.

Leaders who practice the United Methodist way are called to "recommend fasting or abstinence, both by precept and example."

Question Seventeen: Are you determined to employ all your time in the work of God?

What is the work of God? In question five we examined some
dynamics that are integral in understanding the work of God. It was
stated previously that the work of ministry is to do God's will, and
Jesus has demonstrated to us what it means to do God's will. First,
we are to love our neighbors. Second, Jesus calls us to feed his sheep.
Third, we are to do ministry like Jesus did his ministry, as witnessed
by John's disciples (Luke 7:22):

- The blind receive their sight.
- The lame walk.
- The lepers are cleansed.
- The deaf hear.
- The dead are raised.
- The poor have good news brought to them.

This is one helpful way to describe the work of God. Ordination offers a "yes" to the eighteenth question. One's ordination says that one is willing to devote himself or herself wholly to God and God's work.

Time management is an important consideration in the conduct of one's ministry. We can take a cue from the Preacher: "There's a season for everything / and a time for every matter under the heavens" (Eccles. 3:1). This managed time is bracketed by "a time for giving birth and a time for dying" (Eccles. 3:2).

What is really meant by the notion "employ all your time in the work of God"? Wesley believed that we must keep our focus on God and God's work—body, mind, and spirit. This focus includes nurturing the spiritual disciplines and practicing social holiness. How much time does one spend on doing God's work? We live in a different society from that of Wesley. Wesley spent most of his waking hours doing God's work. Let me suggest that in determining the time spent on doing God's work, we must set priorities.

What are the appropriate priorities of a pilgrim disciple? The following priorities help to keep things in balance and perspective:

- God
- family
- work

By setting these priorities, I believe that a person in ministry can do an ample amount of God's work, but it requires a balance of time and emphasis.

Doing God's work is much more than doing work. It is about living the Christian lifestyle. It is about faith sharing. It is about preaching, teaching, and healing in the name of Jesus. Doing God's work has to do with following Jesus—the way, the truth, the life.

Question Eighteen: Are you in debt so as to embarrass you in your work?

The cost of a theological school education in America today is expensive. Far too many students graduate with significant unpaid student loans. These same graduates will enter into ministry and receive a minimum salary, making it difficult to pay off student loans in a timely manner.

When John Wesley first posed this question, he was concerned about laypeople who entered the ministry with family debts. He could not have foreseen the high cost of theological education in the twenty-first century. Yet his question is right on target. Ministerial debt is a problem in America today for several reasons:

1. Clergy are graduating from seminary with significant unpaid student debts.

2. Too many clergy have become victims of credit card debt, some of which was incurred to get through seminary.

3. Far too many clergy have very poor stewardship habits.

In the first instance, The United Methodist Church initiated the Ministerial Education Fund to assist with the ever-rising cost of theological education. The idea was to provide funds to augment the budgets of our United Methodist theological schools. A portion of the Ministerial Education funds are retained by the annual conferences and administered by the various conference boards of ordained ministry. Each annual conference decides how to use its funds; however, many conferences award scholarships to their theological school students.

It is important for annual conferences to pay their Ministerial Education Fund apportionment in full as a means of supporting our seminarians and reducing the amount of debt incurred by our students. Pastoral leaders have the opportunity to lead congregations in attaining such a worthy goal.

A second concern is the matter of poor stewardship practices among our clergy. Clergy must be students of stewardship and money, learning how to manage money, especially their own money. How do we care for the gifts that God gives to us to manage?

In his sermon "The Use of Money," John Wesley provides cogent principles regarding the use of money: "Having first gained all you can, and secondly saved all you can then give all you can." Consider some of Wesley's principles:

- We ought not gain money at the expense of life.
- We are to gain all we can without hurting our minds any more than our bodies.
- We are to gain all we can without hurting our neighbor.
- Gain all you can, by common sense, by using in your business all the understanding that God has given you.
- Do not throw it away in idle expenses. (In other words, do not waste your money on things, especially self-gratification.)
- Give all you have, as well as all you are, a spiritual sacrifice to Him who withheld not from you his Son.[1]

Wesley wanted his "helpers" to be stewardship practitioners.

Here are a few tips for people in ministry, especially local church pastors:

- Know the value of money.
- Learn to give and to receive.
- Live within your means.

- Be a stewardship practitioner.
- Do not borrow money from friends and parishioners.
- Do not sign checks or hold any church money.
- Delegate all financial duties to the laity.

The idea is that money will not be allowed to become your nemesis because of debt or fraud.

Question Nineteen: Will you observe the following directions?

a. Be diligent. Never be unemployed. Never be triflingly employed. Never trifle away time; neither spend any more time at any one place than is strictly necessary.

b. Be punctual. Do everything exactly at the time. And do not mend our rules, but keep them; not for wrath, but for conscience' sake.

What does it mean to be diligent? A diligent minister is one who is constant in his or her effort to accomplish the work of ministry. The person's work is characterized by attentiveness, persistence, and perseverance. One can experience great joy and satisfaction in doing the work of ministry. Commitment to Christ is the foundation that enables those who are willing to commit all their time in doing the work of God. Wesley wanted his helpers to give their full and devoted attention to God's work. He was diligent in doing God's work, and he expected others to be just as committed. The word *diligent* can be found in use throughout Wesley's written materials.

Wesley admonishes us never to be unemployed because we are to be doing God's work. When called to ministry and God's work, the minister is to be employed in the work of ministry. For elders and deacons in The United Methodist Church, this means full-time employment, unless otherwise stated in an agreement. An issue confronting The United Methodist Church today is underemployment, the underutilization of a person's skills or capacity for ministry. A person who has pastoral responsibility for fewer than one hundred parishioners is probably engaged in underemployment in that pastoral appointment. The time, energy, and spiritual capacity of a pastor or deacon should be used fully in his or her ministry assignment.

Wesley was so concerned about the work of a person in ministry that he admonishes us here not to be triflingly employed. A person who is triflingly employed is doing work or ministry that is lacking in significance or solid worth. The church's ministry for Wesley was significant and of great worth. The lesson here is always to stay focused on ministry and mission. Wesley wanted his preachers to spend time reading. One must read, meditate, and pray daily. Without this approach, Wesley believed that one could not be a "deep preacher," or a "thorough Christian." He said: "Fix some part of every day for private exercises." He concluded, "[E]lse you will be a trifler all your days."[1]

Time is an important factor in ministry, and it should never be trifled away or wasted in idleness. We are to use our time wisely and judiciously. There are twenty-four hours in a day, so there is ample time to do the work of ministry. We must set our priorities and faithfully use the time that is granted to us. We can do this by setting priorities, and doing only what is essential. There is no place for a lazy person in ministry!

One way to avoid trifling away time is to avoid spending "more time at any one place than is strictly necessary." A rule of thumb here is not to hang out with your friends in the parish or community. There is a time and a place for hanging out with friends. The minister's priority is to visit from place to place and home to home. Care for souls appropriately, and move on to the next place.

In the matter of time management, John Wesley further admonishes us to be punctual. The late Bishop Prince Albert Taylor use to say that "if you are not in your seat five minutes before it is time for a meeting to start, you are late." Start early and allow ample time so that you can be on time. When we "do everything exactly at the time," it teaches our parishioners to know that they can expect things to begin on time. It helps the spiritual leader to be ready because he or she has made advance preparation.

Wesley's final counsel in this nineteenth question is absolute: And do not mend our rules, but keep them; not for wrath, but for conscience' sake.

POSTSCRIPT

Methodist preachers have been required to answer the Historic Questions from the beginning of Methodism. The questions are posed to persons who are about to be ordained as elders and become full members of an annual conference. The actual questions were formulated by John Wesley with their origin in the questions that Wesley posed to the early Methodist laypeople. There has been very little change in the questions over the years.

In *The Book of Discipline, 2012*[1] you will find a historic examination that is used with candidates who are admitted into full connection and ordained as deacons. A review of that list of questions indicates that there are some minor differences from the Historic Questions used with a candidate who is seeking to be ordained as elder. One notable difference is question thirteen: "Will you exercise the ministry of compassion?"

It is important to remember that the first Historic Question asks, "Have you faith in Christ?" This is the very question to which we should return as we end this conversation: Do you have faith in Christ?

Does your deep and abiding faith in Christ provide for you a sure foundation that undergirds your living the United Methodist way?

The United Methodist way is a disciplined life. It is like the Benedictine Rule that has three vows:

- obedience
- stability
- conversion in the way of life

Be guided by Jesus, who said, "I am the way, I am the truth, I am the life."

As a minister in The United Methodist Church, always celebrate the fact that the best thing that has ever happened to you is that you fell in love with Jesus. His arms of protection will surround you as you go into the world

- to reform the nation
- to reform the church
- to spread scriptural holiness throughout the land

In the conduct of your ministry, continue to grapple with the questions; live the questions now, and you will live your way into God's answers.

A Covenant Prayer in the Wesleyan Tradition

I am no longer my own, but thine.
Put me to what thou wilt, rank me with whom thou wilt.
Put me to doing, put me to suffering.
Let me be employed by thee or laid aside for thee,
exalted for thee or brought low for thee.
Let me be full, let me be empty.
Let me have all things, let me have nothing.
I freely and heartily yield all things

to thy pleasure and disposal.
And now, O glorious and blessed God,
Father, Son, and Holy Spirit,
thou art mine, and I am thine. So be it.
And the covenant which I have made on earth,
let it be ratified in heaven. Amen.[2]

NOTES

Live the Questions Now

1. Rainer Maria Rilke, *Letters to a Young Poet* (New York: W. W. Norton, 1934), 34–35.

Introduction

1. John Wesley, "Letters, Essays, Dialogs and Addresses / Some Remarks on 'A Defense of Aspasio Vindicated,'" in *The Works of John Wesley*, ed. Thomas Jackson, 14 vols., CD-ROM edition (Franklin, TN: Providence House, 1994), 10: 352; hereafter cited as *Works* (Jackson).

2. Frederick A. Norwood, ed., *The Methodist Discipline of 1798, Including the Annotations of Thomas Coke and Francis Asbury*, facsimile edition (Rutland, VT: Academy Books, 1979), 66.

3. Richard P. Heitzenrater, *Wesley and the People Called Methodists* (Nashville: Abingdon Press, 2008), 308.

4. Rueben Job, *Three Simple Rules: A Wesleyan Way of Living* (Nashville: Abingdon Press, 2007), 10.

5. Hoyt L. Hickman, ed., "The Summons," in *The Faith We Sing*, (Nashville: Abingdon Press, 2000), 2130.

6. Wesley, "The Life of the Rev. John Wesley," in *Works* (Jackson): 5:524.

Question One

1. John Wesley, "Feb. 1, 1737–38 to Sept. 16, 1738," *Journals and Diaries, I (1735–38)*, ed. W. Reginald Ward and Richard P. Heitzenrater, vol. 18

of *The Bicentennial Edition of the Works of John Wesley* (Nashville: Abingdon Press, 1988), 228.

2. Wesley, "Journal from October 14, 1735 to February 1, 1737–38," in *Works* (Jackson), 1:103.

3. John Wesley, Sermon 106, "On Faith," in *Sermons III*, ed. Albert C. Outler, vol. 3 of *The Bicentennial Edition of the Works of John Wesley* (Nashville: Abingdon Press, 1986).

4. John Wesley, Sermon 117, "On the Discoveries of Faith," in *Sermons IV*, ed. Albert C. Outler, vol. 4 of *The Bicentennial Edition of the Works of John Wesley* (Nashville: Abingdon Press, 1987), 35.

5. Wesley, Sermon 106, "On Faith"—Hebrews 11:6, 3:497–98.

Question Two

1. Wesley, Sermon 40, "Christian Perfection," in *Sermons II,* ed. Albert C. Outler, vol. 2 of *The Bicentennial Edition of the Works of John Wesley* (Nashville: Abingdon Press, 1985), 104.

2. Ibid.

3. Albert C. Outler, ed., *John Wesley* (New York: Oxford University Press, 1964), 284.

4. Wesley, Sermon 92, "On Zeal," in *Works* (Jackson), 3:313–14.

Question Three

1. John Wesley, "May 6, 1760 to October 28, 1762," *Journal and Diaries IV (1755–65),* ed. W. Reginald Ward and Richard P. Heitzenrater, vol. 21 of *The Bicentennial Edition of the Works of John Wesley* (Nashville: Abingdon Press, 1992), 389.

2. "O Perfect Love," in *The United Methodist Hymnal* (Nashville: The United Methodist Publishing House, 1989), 645.

3. Ibid., "Love Divine, All Loves Excelling," 384.

4. Wesley, "A Plain Account of Christian Perfection as Believed and Taught by the Reverend Mr. John Wesley, from the Year, 1725 to the Year 1777," in *Works* (Jackson): 11:371.

5. Wesley, Sermon 16: "The Means of Grace," in *Sermons I,* ed. Albert C. Outler, vol. 1 of *The Bicentennial Edition of the Works of John Wesley* (Nashville: Abingdon Press, 1984), 381.

6. Wesley, Sermon 92, "On Zeal," in *Sermons III,* ed. Albert C. Outler,

vol. 3 of *The Bicentennial Edition of the Works of John Wesley* (Nashville: Abingdon Press, 1986), 313.

Question Four

1. Joseph E. Lowery, *Singing the Lord's Song in a Strange Land* (Nashville: Abingdon Press, 2011), 71.

2. Wesley, Sermon 85, "On Working Out Our Own Salvation," in *Sermons III*, ed., Albert C. Outler, vol. 3 of *The Bicentennial Edition of the Works of John Wesley* (Nashville: Abingdon Press, 1986), 202.

Question Five

1. Wesley, "Addresses, Essays, Letters/Minutes of Several Conversations Between the Rev. Mr. Wesley and Others," in *Works* (Jackson), 8:300.

2. Jefferson Cleveland and Verolga Nix, eds., *Songs of Zion* (Nashville: Abingdon Press, 1981), 146.

Question Six

1. Marjorie J. Thompson, *Soul Feast: An Invitation to the Christian Spiritual Life* (Louisville, KY: Westminster John Knox Press, 1995), 146.

2. From *The Book of Discipline of The United Methodist Church, 2012*. Copyright © 2012 by The United Methodist Publishing House; 75–78. Used by permission.

Question Seven

1. *The United Methodist Hymnal* (Nashville: The United Methodist Publishing House, 1989), 562.

2. John Wesley, "Upon Our Lord's Sermon on the Mount, VI," Sermons 1–33, in *Sermons I*, ed., Albert C, Outler, vol. 1 of *The Bicentennial Edition of the Works of John Wesley* (Nashville: Abingdon Press, 1984), 573.

Question Eight

1. From *The Book of Discipline of The United Methodist Church, 2012*. Copyright © 2012 by The United Methodist Publishing House, 45–89. Used by permission.

2. Ibid., 102, Section 1–"Our Doctrinal Heritage," 45.

3. Ibid., 47–48.

4. Ibid., ¶ 102.49.

5. Ibid., 49–52.

6. Wesley, "Thoughts Upon Methodism," in *Works* (Jackson), 13:259.

Question Nine

1. From *The Book of Discipline of The United Methodist Church, 2012*. Copyright © 2012 by The United Methodist Publishing House; ¶ 105, Section 4—"Our Theological Task, Theological Guidelines: Sources and Criteria," 80–86. Used by permission.

2. Ibid., "The Articles of Religion," Article V, "Of the Sufficiency of the Holy Scriptures for Salvation," 64–65.

3. Ibid., "The Confession of Faith of The Evangelical United Brethren Church," Article IV, 71.

4. Wesley, Sermons 1–33.; Preface and Introduction, in *Sermons I*, ed. Albert C. Outler, vol. 1 of *The Bicentennial Edition of the Works of John Wesley* (Nashville: Abingdon Press, 1984), 105–6.

5. Wesley, "Minutes of Several Conversations Between the Rev. Mr. Wesley and Others, 1744–1789," in *Works* (Jackson), 8:315.

Question Eleven

1. John Wesley, Sermon 107, "On God's Vineyard," in *Sermons III*, ed. Albert C. Outler, vol. 3 of *The Bicentennial Edition of the Works of John Wesley* (Nashville Abingdon Press, 1986), 511.

Question Twelve

1. From *The Book of Discipline of The United Methodist Church, 2012*. Copyright © 2012 by The United Methodist Publishing House; ¶ 120, "The Mission," 91. Used by permission.

2. Ibid., ¶ 121, "Rationale for Our Mission," 91.

Question Thirteen

1. From *The Book of Discipline of The United Methodist Church, 2012*. Copyright © 2012 by The United Methodist Publishing House; ¶ 201.143. Used by permission.

2. Ibid., ¶ 202.143.

3. Ibid.

Question Fourteen

1. *The New National Baptist Hymnal* (Nashville: National Baptist Publishing Board, 1977), 470.

Question Fifteen

1. Wesley, "Addresses, Essays, Letters, Minutes of Several Conversations Between the Rev. Mr. Wesley and Others," in *Works* (Jackson): 8:300.

Question Sixteen

1. Wesley, Sermon 27, "Sermon on the Mount," in *Sermons I*, ed. Albert C. Outler, vol. 1 of *The Bicentennial Edition of the Works of John Wesley* (Nashville: Abingdon Press, 1984), 593–94.

2. Ibid., 595.

3. Ibid.

4. Ibid., 598.

5. Ibid., 600.

6. Ann Weems, "Giving Up for Lent," in *Putting the Amazing Back in Grace* (Louisville, KY: Westminster John Knox Press, 1999), 44.

Question Eighteen

1. Wesley, Sermon 50, "The Use of Money," in *Sermons II*, ed. Albert C. Outler, vol. 2 of *The Bicentennial Edition of the Works of John Wesley* (Nashville: Abingdon Press, 1985), 277.

Question Nineteen

1. Wesley, "Letters from John Wesley to Various Persons," and "Letters to Mr. John Trembath," in *Works* (Jackson), 12:254.

Postscript

1. From *The Book of Discipline of The United Methodist Church, 2012.* Copyright © 2012 by The United Methodist Publishing House; ¶ 330, 5d. "Historic Examination for Admission into Full Connection and Ordination as Deacon," 250–51. Used by permission.

2. *The United Methodist Hymnal* (Nashville: United Methodist Publishing House, 1989), 607.

•

BIBLIOGRAPHY

The Book of Discipline of The United Methodist Church. Nashville: The United Methodist Publishing House, 2008.

Cartwright, Michael G., with Andrew D. Kinsey. *Watching Over One Another in Love: Reclaiming the Wesleyan Rule of Life.* The Indiana Conference of The United Methodist Church, 2010.

Cleveland, Jefferson, and Verolga Nix, eds. *The Songs of Zion.* Nashville: Abingdon Press, 1981.

Dean, Mary Catherine. *The Wesley Study Bible* (New Revised Standard Version). Nashville: Abingdon Press, 2009.

Heitzenrater, Richard P. *Wesley and the People Called Methodists.* Nashville: Abingdon Press, 1995, 2013.

Hickman, Hoyt L., ed. *The Faith We Sing.* Nashville: Abingdon Press, 2000.

Job, Rueben. *Three Simple Rules: A Wesleyan Way of Living.* Nashville: Abingdon Press, 2007.

Lowery, Joseph E. *Singing the Lord's Song in a Strange Land*. Nashville: Abingdon Press, 2011.

Manskar, Steven W. "What Is Wesleyan About Leadership?" *Covenant Discipleship Connection Newsletter,* January 15, 2010. Nashville: General Board of Discipleship. Explores the Historic Questions in this and several subsequent newsletters.

National Baptist Publishing Board. *The New National Baptist Hymnal*. Nashville: National Baptist Publishing Board, 1977.

Norwood, Frederick A., ed. *The Methodist Discipline of 1798, Including the Annotations of Thomas Coke and Francis Asbury.* Facsimile edition. Rutland, VT: Academy Books, 1979.

Outler, Albert C., ed. *John Wesley*. New York: Oxford University Press, 1964.

Rhude, Beth E. *"Live the Questions Now: The Interior Life.* New York: Women's Division, Board of Global Ministries, 1980.

Rilke, Rainer Maria. *"Letters to a Young Poet*. New York: W. W. Norton, 1934.

Thompson, Marjorie J. *Soul Feast: An Invitation to the Christian Spiritual Life*. Louisville, KY: Westminster John Knox Press, 1995.

The United Methodist Hymnal. Nashville: The United Methodist Publishing House, 1989.

Weems, Ann. *Putting the Amazing Back in Grace*. Louisville, KY: Westminster John Knox Press, 1999.

Wesley, John. *The Works of John Wesley.* Nashville: Abingdon Press, vols. 1–4 (1984–87), 18 (1988), and 21 (1992) of the Bicentennial Edition.

————. *The Works of John Wesley.* Jackson Edition. Franklin, TN: Providence House Publishers, 1994. CD-ROM.

CPSIA information can be obtained at www.ICGtesting.com
Printed in the USA
LVOW12s1332040215

425695LV00001B/1/P